Weaving &
Spinning

EXCALIBUR BOOKS

Edited by Yvonne Deutch

Published in the United States by
Excalibur Books
201 Park Avenue South
New York, New York 10003

© Marshall Cavendish Limited 1975, 1976, 1977

First printing 1977

Printed in Great Britain

ISBN 0-525-70070-6

This publication is not to be sold outside of
the U.S.A, Philippine Republic and Canada.

*Above: Materials for
spinning include fleece,
hand carders and a
simple drop spindle.*

Introduction

Weaving and spinning are two of the most ancient crafts, and over the centuries man has inherited a wealth of skills and techniques to use in a modern context. There are few things as satisfying as handling a length of hand-woven fabric, with its individual pattern and texture, especially if you have made it yourself. Today there is a great interest in getting back in touch with our crafts heritage, and weaving and spinning provide the sort of fulfilment that people are seeking in a world that has become increasingly mechanized.

We take the beginner right back to the roots of these crafts in *Weaving and Spinning*, using a gradual build-up of steps, from the simplest procedures right through to the most sophisticated techniques on modern table looms. Step-by-step instructions, attractive illustrations and clear working diagrams enable the most inexperienced weaver to tackle the projects. A whole variety of weaving methods are described, including tablet and inkle weaving. We show you how to make bags, belts, braids, chokers, wall hanging and samplers—even a beautiful jacket woven on a frame loom.

The real enthusiast will want to start from scratch, and learn the basics of spinning. We show you how to spin both with a spindle and a wheel. However, ready-spun yarns in a variety of textures and exquisite colours are readily available, and we recommend those suitable for each project. The way to experience the satisfaction of weaving and spinning is to start now. You'll be rewarded with the pleasure of handling beautiful materials and producing unique creations with your own hands.

Contents

Weaving

Star weaving~ God's Eyes

A primitive form of weaving—star weaving—has in recent years found its way into contemporary decor. These colourful stars are most commonly seen in Latin America though they are also found in Africa and the East. In Latin America they are known as Ojos de Dios – God's Eyes. In Mexico God's Eyes were made to symbolize the eye of a god and were a supplication for help or watchful care from the gods. If more than one God's Eye was woven onto the crossed sticks then it was primarily for the gods to look kindly upon a child. A God's Eye was made for each year of a child's life up to five years—after this the child was supposed to be able to make his own requests. The age of a child could also be represented by the number of colours used.

Today God's Eyes are enjoyed for their use of colour and texture and because they are easy and fun to make. The materials are inexpensive and readily available. This is an excellent opportunity to use up scraps of yarn left over from other work.

Materials

You will need two straight sticks or dowels of about the same length and thickness. You can use sticks from the garden but straight, smooth sticks are the easiest to use to begin with.

When choosing yarn let your imagination run wild with colour combinations. The thickness of the yarn should be relative to the thickness of the sticks, 6mm (¼in) diameter sticks work best with double knitting weight. With practice you will be able to vary the yarn weights on each project.

The yarn may be of any material—wool, cotton or man-made fibres. It is best to use at least two-ply on your first projects as you will be pulling on it to maintain the tension.

Remember – it is always better to have too much yarn rather than not enough, so check your quantities first.

Lashing Lay one stick on top of the other at right angles with centres matching. Lay one end of yarn (in this case orange) diagonally across the intersection of the two sticks. Hold the tail of yarn to the junction of the sticks with your thumb. At the same

These stars are woven with three-ply rug wool. The smaller star is based on curved twigs, and the large star on green split bamboo garden stakes. The stars use both methods of winding, raised and recessed, and the smaller one is decorated with feathers.

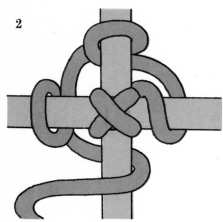

time, hold the junction of the sticks, on the side away from you, with the index and middle finger of the same hand.

With your free hand begin winding the yarn away from you diagonally, holding it taut as you do so. In this way the yarn should cross the sticks diagonally at the junction, on one side and have parallel sides on the other. Wind the yarn diagonally around the crossing point of the sticks alternately to the right and to the left, thus forming an X over the centre of the sticks (fig.1). When the centre wood is totally covered, you have lashed the sticks together to provide a firm core for the star.

Note: remember to pull the yarn taut as you wrap so sticks stay in place and act as a firm support in the centre.

Turn the sticks over and tie a small but tight knot at the centre of the back with the original tail of the yarn and the yarn you now hold in your hand. This secures the lashing. Do not cut the yarn. Turn the sticks over again so that the knot is at the back. The side facing you is from now on the 'right side' of the star. Always work with this side facing you.

Weaving There are two basic methods of wrapping the yarn to make stars. One shows the shape of the sticks (fig.2), the other covers the shape of the sticks completely and is slightly raised (fig.3). In both cases, all wood is covered until the outer edge of the star is reached, and either method gives attractive results.

This example continues with the orange yarn that was used for the lashing, and begins with the method that covers the shape of the sticks completely, providing a raised effect.

Begin by holding the star in one hand and the yarn in the other (with the right side of the star facing you). Carry the orange yarn over one stick so that the yarn lies just next to the last round of lashing. Bring the yarn under the stick and back around the top of the stick (fig.3). (Keep the yarn taut throughout the entire procedure). You have now completed one wrapping.

Carry the yarn forward to the next arm of the star. Again, lay the yarn on top of the stick next to the last round of lashing. Wind the yarn under the stick and around the top of the stick. Don't forget to keep the yarn pulled taut. Continue onto the next arm of the star and finally the fourth arm and back to where you began. You have now completed one round. Repeat this round until you have woven about 2.5cm (1in) from the centre of the star in each direction. You now have the centre of the star completed.

Changing colours You are now ready to change colours. This design changes from orange to purple. On the wrong side of the star stop at one arm and cut the yarn leaving a tail of about 5cm (2in). Loop the tail once round the arm and tuck the end under the

1. Start lashing by making a figure eight around two crossed sticks.
2. Recessed method of wrapping.

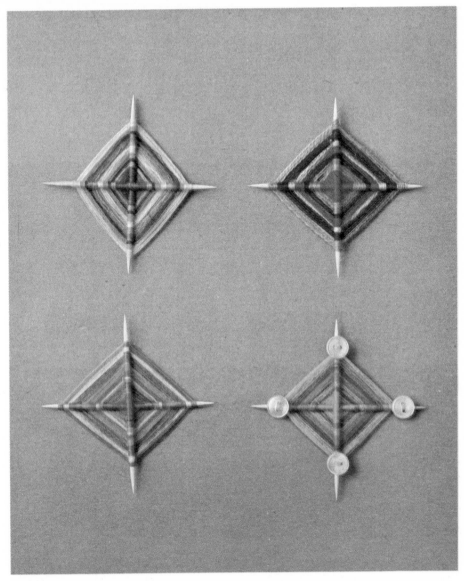

3

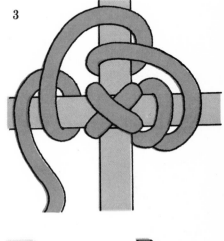

4

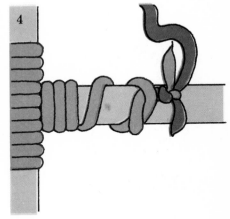

loop. Pull the end tightly. (This will hold the tension of the yarn in place while you join the new colour). Making a double knot, attach the purple yarn to the tail of orange yarn. Tie the knot as close as possible to the arm of the star (fig.4).

Continue wrapping the purple yarn around the arms of the star just as you did with the orange yarn. To follow the example shown, wrap the purple yarn until its width is 12mm ($\frac{1}{2}$in).

Change to the red yarn, following the method for changing colours. After winding the red yarn for 6mm ($\frac{1}{4}$in) in width, change to a blue yarn. With the blue yarn change to the other technique of

3. Raised method of wrapping covers the shape of the sticks.
4. Join a new colour on the wrong side of the stick with a tight knot.

wrapping the yarn (fig.2). You will note that the blue area appears to be recessed. This is due to the second wrapping technique which shows the shapes of the sticks.

Begin by wrapping the blue yarn under the nearest arm of the star. Now bring the yarn around the top of the stick and around the underside again. Carry the yarn to the next arm and repeat the first two steps (fig.2). The blue yarn is wrapped for a width of 12mm ($\frac{1}{2}$in.) Now, change back to the orange yarn and wrap it for a width of 6mm ($\frac{1}{4}$in), following the same methods.

Then change to a yellow yarn and resume the original method of wrapping (going over the stick, then under and back over). Continue this method to near the end of the sticks. The yellow yarn is wound for a width of 6mm ($\frac{1}{4}$in). Then wind the rose yarn for 18mm ($\frac{3}{4}$in); purple for 12mm ($\frac{1}{2}$in); orange for 12mm ($\frac{1}{2}$in) and finally purple for 18mm ($\frac{3}{4}$in).

Finally, on the wrong side, knot the purple yarn with an overhand knot. If you wish to cover the longer bottom arm of the star, as has been done in this model, do not cut the purple yarn close to the knot after you have finished weaving the star, but instead wrap the yarn around and around the stick until you reach the end. Then make your overhand knot on the wrong side of the stick.

Decorating stars

You may leave your star as it is, or further embellish it with various ornaments The most common practice is to hang things from the exposed ends of the arms. You may, however, wish to sew or weave objects onto the face of the weaving. Tassels, pompons, feathers, bows, buttons, seashells and beads can all be used.

As you become more proficient at making stars, you may want to try something more challenging. Some methods of varying stars are: Irregular sticks will add bumps and concave areas to the wrapping. The sticks can be bumpy and/or curved to add interest. Just remember that these irregularities make it more difficult to maintain the tension and will require extra attention. Very long, fat, short or thin sticks all give different looks to your stars.

Besides changing colours with yarn, you may also like to try changing textures. There are all sorts of novelty yarns on the market, some giving a bumpy or looped effect. A smooth cotton followed by a bumpy, novelty yarn could give a dramatic effect.

Mobiles made with God's Eyes add a new dimension to a room. Children are attracted to them because of the lively colours. You can even use very tiny stars (made with wooden tooth picks for the cross pieces and very fine wool or cotton) to hang on the Christmas tree. They add colour in an original way.

Finger weaving

Finger weaving is a process of making woven cloth by using your fingers to guide the wefts through the warp ends. As well as being the simplest form of weaving it is also thought to be the oldest. Examples of ancient braids woven by this method have been found in almost every part of the world. People in places as far apart as Peru, Egypt and Scandinavia worked out patterns by manipulating various colours of yarn with their fingers.

Finger weaving travels well! Because you need no tools, it is the ideal pastime while travelling or sitting in the garden or on the beach, you can carry all your materials with you.

The easiest patterns to make in finger weaving are diagonal bands of colour. From this basic method wavy lines of colour can be woven as illustrated. Once the principle of separating the warp ends and inserting the wefts has been achieved, chevron and diamond patterns can be worked by grouping the yarn differently and weaving it in two directions. And so the progression towards the complex grouping of yarns to produce double woven braids in an infinite variety of patterns and colours, is easy.

Use the braids for decorating sweaters and woollen dresses, for making into belts, book markers, cuffs, napkin rings, watchstraps, chokers, bracelets, hatbands and sashes.

Braid widths Although finger weaving is primarily useful for weaving narrow bands using about 16 strands, wider pieces can be made – with practice. The maximum number of strands which can be handled comfortably is about 48, however the width of the finished braid will depend on the thickness of the yarn. Narrow bands may be sewn together to make either wide bands of colour, wall hangings, place mats, cushions, shopping-, shoulder -or hand-bags. Braids can also be joined by working several braids simultaneously and intertwining the outside strands of each set.

The materials needed for finger weaving are simple and inexpensive. All you need is yarn – rug wool, knitting wool or cotton or synthetic yarn – and a pencil to which to attach the yarn. Use double knitting yarn to begin with as this is the simplest to use. After learning the skill of finger weaving, interesting effects can be

An assortment of colourful braids

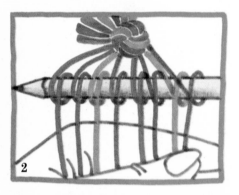

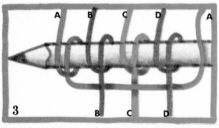

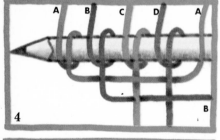

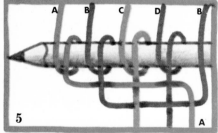

produced by using heavy wools and string or fine silks and cottons. **Colour** is fundamental to weaving and the choice of colour combinations should be given some thought before a project is started. When choosing colour schemes for braids to decorate clothes, choose one colour which picks up or matches the colour of the garment. Experiment with colours and combinations of colour because the play of colour can be one of the most exciting parts of your work and reflects your individual style.

Finger weaving relies heavily on the use of colour contrasts. Strong contrasts produce a bold effect and accentuate the pattern, while subtle combinations create a softer mood and give a more subtle pattern which can be equally effective. Alternatively, use a small amount of a neutral colour to 'break up' bands of primary colours. Sections of three or four colours containing six, seven or eight strands give an effective result although more or less can be used. To make a belt or anything else which needs to have a fringe at either end, set up as follows:

Cutting the yarn Cut the various coloured yarns into the required number of lengths. Each length of yarn should be two or three times as long as the finished length of the article, depending on how long you wish the fringe to be. If you wish to hem the ends, then twice the length is ample. For example, if you are weaving something 15cm (6in) long, cut the yarn 30cm (12in) long. The width of the finished braid will be about $\frac{1}{2}$-$\frac{3}{4}$ of the width of the yarn wound around the pencil and squeezed together.

First of all anchor the yarn firmly to some immovable object by tying an overhand knot at one end of the bunch of yarns and looping over a hook, door knob, chair or drawer handle (fig.1,) or by pinning them securely to a cork board. Wind each strand in turn around a pencil, about 5cm (2in) below the knot, (fig.2).

Weaving

Set the strands onto the pencil in groups of colour, arranging them side by side. Hold the strands towards you about 8cm (3in) below the pencil in the right hand. (These lengths of yarn are called the warp ends.) As the threads are used, pass them to your left hand and hold taut to keep the work firm.

Working from left to right, pick up strand A and weave it under strand B, over strand C, under strand D and so on across all the strands (fig.3). Pull strand A parallel to the pencil and, using the forefinger of the left hand, push it up close to the pencil. Tuck strand A over the right end of the pencil.

Pick up strand B and weave it under strand C, over strand D, under the next and so on across all the strands. You may find it easier to think of the weaving movement as plaiting [braiding] the travelling strand across (fig.4). It is a very simple movement.

Pull strand B parallel to the pencil and push it against the pencil. Remember to push up the strands after they have been carried through the warp ends. The pattern and tension can then be checked for evenness and corrected before the pattern has progressed too far for you to adjust your work.

To make a selvedge on the right hand side, bring strand A either under or over strand B (whichever completes the weaving sequence) and place it parallel to the other warp ends. Tuck strand B over the pencil. The method of making the selvedge is the same for whatever pattern you are weaving (fig.5).

Pick up strand C and weave it under the second warp end, over the third, under the fourth and so on across the warp ends. Continue weaving each warp end on the far left, using it as a weft, through the warp ends, always reversing the sequence of the previous row and bringing every weft down over or under the lower one to complete the selvedge on the right hand side (fig.5).

Make sure the strands aren't getting tangled – sort them out as you go along. Pull each horizontal strand firmly but not too tightly and give the warp ends a gentle straightening pull after each movement. **The horizontal strands should be completely covered by the warp** ends. Check to make sure that they are.

For the first five or ten minutes it will probably seem like a lot of strands and nothing effective happening. Then suddenly you begin to build up rhythm to achieve an even tension and the diagonal pattern starts to grow under your fingers. From that moment on you'll be hooked!

Make sure that you pull the right selvedge firmly, in a straight line. Otherwise the band will begin to curve. (Of course, you can turn this into a virtue when you are making a collar or a hatband.) If you want a fringe at the end of the braid leave 20cm-25cm (8in-10in) of warp ends for finishing the work.

For diagonal stripes set the threads in groups. Following the weaving process, working always from left to right.

For wavy line stripes arrange the strands as for diagonal stripes and follow the weaving process. The same method is followed as given for diagonal stripes, until all the warp ends have been used once as a weft, and the pattern is completed.

Then complete the selvedge on the right hand side and, with the last weft that you used, weave it in and out of the warp ends from right to left. Pick up the far right warp end and weave it in and out, working from right to left also.

To make the selvedge on the left hand side, bring the upper weft

The illustrations opposite show how to weave over a pencil.
1. Anchor yarn firmly.
2. Wind strands around pencil.
3. Weave A from left to right.
4. Weave B from left to right.
5. Bring over B to make selvedge.

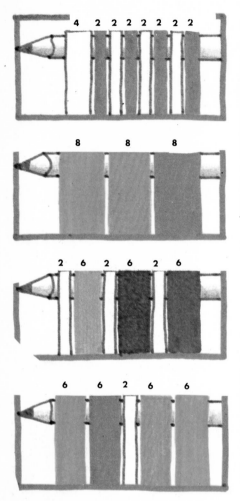

Above: Numerals on diagrams
indicate number of strands needed
to give pattern shown.
Red and white diagonal stripes
Diagonal candy-coloured stripes
Wavy lines with strands of white
Red and white diagonal stripes

either under or over the lower weft (whichever completes the sequence) and place it parallel to the warp ends. Continue in this way, working from right to left, until you want the bands of colour to curve in the reverse direction. If you wish, the change in direction may be made at any point, but the largest curves are achieved by using all the warp ends as wefts before changing direction.

For a chevron pattern choose an even number of colours and strands. Divide each pile into two groups, with the same sequence of colours, and mount them on a pencil so that when the warp ends are divided in the middle the colour sequence of one group is reflected exactly in the other group.

Grip the left group of warp ends in your left hand and the right group in your right hand. Then, using the forefinger and thumb of your right hand, pick up the first warp end at the right edge of the left group. This will become the weft.

Weave this warp end (which is now the weft) over, under, over the warp ends in the right hand. Pull the weft parallel to the pencil. Grasp all the warp ends in the right group in your right hand except the one on the far left of this group. Pass this warp end (now the weft) over, under, over, working from right to left through the warp ends held in the left hand.

Return to the right group of warp ends and pass the far right warp end from the left group over, under, over the warp ends held in the right hand. Repeat this movement with the left group, by passing the far left warp end from the right group over, under, over through the left group of warp ends. Form a selvedge on the right and left sides (fig.5) as you go.

Continue weaving from the centre to the edges until the colour you started with on the far left and far right is positioned in the centre of the warp ends. You have now worked one chevron pattern. Continue in this way until you have worked the required length.

For a chevron pattern with diamond shape mount the strands of yarn on a pencil by tying them halfway along their length in the same sequence as for chevron pattern.

Tie one lot of warp ends in a loose knot – to keep them out of the way while you are weaving the others. Using the free strands, work

Below: Numerals on diagrams indicate number of strands needed to give patterns shown.
Chevron pattern in four colours
Alternating chevron pattern
Chevrons reversed to make diamond pattern

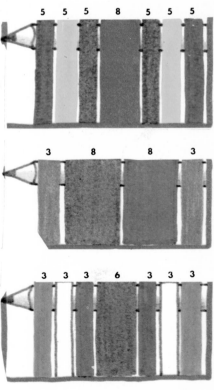

the required length in the chevron pattern. Untie the loose knot and the knots around the pencil. Turn the work around, but not over, so the unworked ends are towards you and weave chevron patterns as before. Because you are working in the opposite direction, a diamond shape is formed in the centre.

Finishing A neat finish enhances any braid.

Plaits [Braids] If the number of warp ends are multiples of three, plait [braid] sets of three warp ends. Knot the ends and trim them.

Ply Take a pair of warp ends. Twist one warp end between your thumb and forefinger to the right until it is very tightly twisted and begins to kink even when held fairly taut. Secure the end with a pin to a cushion or stick it to a table with cellophane tape so it can't unwind. Repeat the twisting with the other warp end and hold it firmly. Pick up the first twisted warp end and hold it firmly too. Hold both warp ends together between your thumb and forefinger and tug firmly while rolling the warp ends towards the left. Release the warp ends. They should twist together, that is, form a ply.

Knots Finish braids and ply by tying knots across the bottom of the sets of braided and plied strands. To make a small knot, take only one of the strands, wrap it round two strands, make a single knot and pull tight. Trim the strands below the knots.

Hems Tie strands in pairs with a double knot and trim ends as close as possible to the knots without weakening them. Turn the knotted ends in 6mm ($\frac{1}{4}$in) to the wrong side and fold again 18mm ($\frac{3}{4}$in) from the edge. Using the same coloured yarn, make neat stab stitches through the braid to prevent the ends from unfolding.

The pretty choker is about 18mm ($\frac{3}{4}$in) wide and 38cm (15in) long, including 5cm (2in) for finishing. Adjust the length according to your requirements by working a little more or a little less.

Choose yarn in four colours and cut into 76cm (30in) lengths, in the quantities given in the diagram.

Mount the centre of each length of yarn on a pencil in the sequence indicated and tie the warp ends that you are not working with in a loose knot. Work 19cm ($7\frac{1}{2}$in) in a chevron pattern. Untie the loose knot and the knots around the pencil. Turn the unworked warp ends around, but not over, and continue with the chevron pattern until the length is 38cm (15in).

Hem both ends of the braid.

Make a fastening by sewing a 12mm ($\frac{1}{2}$in) button to the right side of the band near one edge. Make a loop at the other edge by passing a 10cm (4in) strand of yarn through the folded hem. Knot the two ends together, adjusting to the right length. Trim the ends and thread the knot inside the hem so that it is hidden. The loop will then fasten over the button and secure the band.

Ply, braid and small knot finishes.

Weaving on a simple loom

You now know some simple ways of using yarn – how to weave around a rigid structure with the God's Eyes and how to weave peasant braids on your fingers. To move into weaving 'proper' is not the daunting step that many people believe. Weaving is quite simply the interlacing of two sets of threads, usually at right angles to one another, to form a fabric.

Most people have done some simple weaving at some time – like darning a hole in a sock. This involves setting up a set of threads in one direction (the warp) and darning another thread (the weft) over and under the warp threads, backwards and forwards, until the darn is completed (fig.1). A new piece of cloth has been made and this process is the basis of all weaving.

Usually in darning a sock it is helpful to stretch the warp threads over a 'mushroom' as it is much easier to work if the threads are under tension. A loom is a device which keeps warp threads in tension so that they are easy to weave.

Many people are discouraged from weaving as a craft by the idea that a loom is necessarily a piece of equipment about the size and price of a four-poster bed and needing a special room to house it. Such looms are used, of course, but many of the world's top weavers use nothing more complicated than a picture frame.

Looms

Traditional looms Since the very first piece of weaving was made, many ways have been found of holding the threads in tension. Threads were hung from branches and weighted with stones (fig.2) or stretched between the two ends of a pliable stick (fig.3). The primitive back-strap loom was used to great effect by the pre-Columbian Indians of Peru. Here the tension of the warp threads is achieved by moving the body backwards against the strap (fig.4).

Improvised looms There are many items around the house which will serve as temporary looms for early experiments. Anything with a pair of parallel bars can be used including such everyday objects as a clothes horse (fig.5), landing rails (fig.6), an embroidery slate frame (fig.7) or even the legs of an upturned chair.

Top: A fine example of a pictorial tapestry.
Above: Colour and weave sampler.

17

1 *Interlacement of threads*

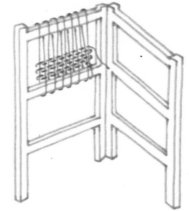

5 *Clothes horse as an improvised loom*

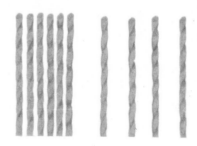

8 *Spacing the warp threads*

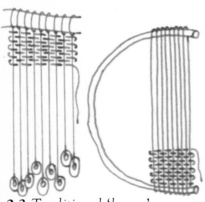

2,3 *Traditional 'looms'. Stones used to weight warps and a pliable branch.*

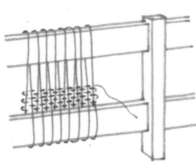

6 *Landing rails*

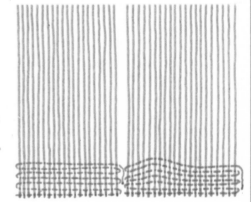

9 *Slack warp threads result in uneven tension.*

4 *Detail of a Peruvian vase showing one of the oldest forms of loom – the back-strap.*

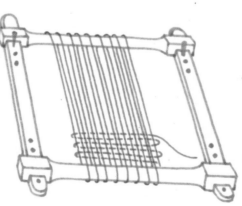

7 *Embroidery slate frame*

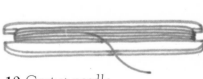

10 *Carpet needle*
11 *Stick shuttle*

The warp threads

The next chapter on weaving deals more fully with materials, but a general rule in choosing a yarn for the warp threads (or 'ends') is that it must be strong but not fluffy or too elastic. Weft threads (or 'picks') can be almost anything as they do not have to take the strains and stresses of the warp threads.

Spacing the warp threads When putting a warp onto these simple looms the threads should be placed very carefully and evenly. A rule of thumb guide is to be able to see more thread than space in between the threads, judged over the area where the weaving is to take place (fig.8). This is a very basic principle in weaving.

To keep the threads evenly spaced, a narrow strip of corrugated cardboard can be taped to the top and bottom edges of the frame. If a thick yarn is being used, one warp thread per groove may be enough, or several thinner threads can occupy one groove. This is a good example of improvising materials for your work.

Even tension

The warp threads on the simple loom are created by winding a continuous thread around the loom, knotting the thread securely to the frame at beginning and end. When winding the warp threads around the loom, it is helpful to wind in a figure eight.

Do not let any of the warp threads cross over another thread. Try also to keep all the threads at the same tension – comfortably taut. To test them before weaving, close your eyes (this helps to concentrate the sense of touch) and pat your hand across the warp from one side to the other. Tighten up those threads which are slack by moving the yarn around the loom or by padding with wads of paper between the threads and the frame.

Almost all weaving needs an evenly-tensioned warp. Areas which are slacker than the rest of the warp will show in the weaving (fig.9), and spoil the effect of the finished work.

Starting to weave

On more elaborate looms, there will be mechanical help in lifting every other thread, but on simple looms the weft can be put through with a large packing or carpet needle (fig.10). If a large piece is being woven, then a stick shuttle is useful (fig.11). This holds long lengths of weft yarn as well as acting as a needle for darning in and out of the threads.

Placing the weft Start the weft, darning across from one side leaving an 8cm (3in) tail hanging. This is woven in for about 2.5cm (1in) when the weft is taken from that side next time. Do not pull the weft tightly when it reaches the other side of the warp or the

---

Decorative band

You will need:
One ball of 3-ply jute garden twine for both warp and weft. Twine is sold in 450g (1lb) balls but for this length of band 113g (¼lb) is ample.
Carpet needle with large eye.
Any of the improvised looms mentioned above which allows the warp to be 30cm (12in) longer than the length of the band. The example was woven between two table legs.

Below: The pattern on the band is made by weaving alternate thicknesses of twine.

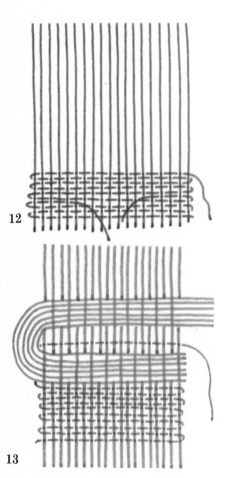

fabric will curve in at the edges where the threads may eventually break under the strain. Try to get into the habit of gently pulling the weft snugly against the selvedge before beating down.

Beating The weft thread has to be pressed gently but firmly into place and a table fork or coarse hair comb can be helpful.

Joining a weft thread To join on a new length of weft thread, either start at the edge (as the first weft pick was started) or overlap with the new thread for about 4cm (1½in). When changing colour it is usually (fig.12) better to start at the edge. Avoid knots anywhere in both warp and weft since they spoil the surface.

Tie one end of three-ply to the lower bar of the loom. Wind the warp in a figure eight up around the top bar of the loom and back again around the lower bar until you have 19 warp threads. If a wider band is required, increase the number of threads to any odd number until you achieve the width you want.

It is important to remember that the warp should be at least 30cm (12in) longer than the length of the finished article.

Using the carpet needle, start to weave with one strand of three-ply jute about 90cm (3ft) long. Lifting up every other warp thread with the needle, draw the weft through.

The opening provided by the figure eight winding will help in the weaving of every other weft. Beat the weft firmly into position. When you have woven about ten rows of the one strand, leave the strand hanging at the end of a row.

Take six long strands of jute and thread through the needle. Weave one row leaving the ends of the six strands in a tuft as they will be too thick to weave in. Beat the six strands firmly into position. Leave the six strands hanging at the end of the one row of weaving and pick up the one strand.

Weave one row with the one strand. Pick up the six-strand group and weave it back for one row (fig. 13). Weave alternate lengths of the one-strand and the six-strand group to produce the patterned effect. You are now ready to finish the work.

Decorative band

This decorative band for a hat or belt is 3cm (1¼in) wide.

Finish the band with ten rows of one-strand weaving so that the band will be firm when taken off the loom. Weave in the end thread as you did the first thread.

When you have finished the band, cut the warp threads at each end of the band near to the loom bars. Trim the fringe to the required length. If your weaving has been even, the band should remain firm even with a short stubby fringe at both ends.

If attaching to a hat, sew on with tiny stitches.

12. *Joining a new length of weft thread, or pick, into the weaving.*
13. *Weaving the band.*

Shoulder bag

A 23cm by 20cm (9in by 8in) bag with a 52cm (20in) braided strap.
Wind the warp right around the book, knotting the two ends firmly to their adjacent threads.

Start off each weft thread by leaving a tail of 30cm-35cm (12in-14in) at the bottom of the book. Weave up to the top of the book and back down again, leaving another tail at the bottom (fig.14). Weave right around the book, including the spine and the paper edge, although these areas will be covered by the handles.

When the weaving is complete, slide the book out and join the bag up at the bottom by knotting each pair of weft ends with the pair woven on the other side. Join the ends very securely.

The strap Cut 18 1.8m (2yd) lengths of yarn. Make two three-strand plaits each with nine strands. Stitch plaits [braids] to bag.

Shoulder bag

You will need :
200g (½lb) weight of thrums (short lengths) of carpet wool which can be purchased from any carpet factory. Thrums come in irregular lengths and are often 3½m-5½m (12ft-18ft) long. You will need one long length for the warp and shorter lengths for the weft.
Hard-backed book. The one used for the example was 25cm by 20cm (10in by 8in).
Carpet needle.
33m (36yd) of yarn for strap.

The woven shoulder bag with its 'loom', a hard-backed book.

Yarns and fabrics

Materials which are suitable for weaving can be found in a much wider range than is suggested by the yarn suppliers' list. Almost any substance which is obtainable in a long flexible length, as well as the yarns which are designed for the purpose, can be used for weaving, and it is fascinating to assess practically any material in terms of its potential use in this craft. For instance, sheet materials such as cloth can be cut into strips and even paper can be used in many different ways.

Fibres

Most weaving materials are made of fibres and some of these are more suitable than others for certain types of work. The properties of each material have to be carefully considered.

A yarn is made by twisting many individual fibres together (the twist adds strength) and the resulting 'singles' yarn can then be plied or twisted with similar singles to form a two-, three or more ply yarn (fig.1).

The fibres from which yarns are made include vegetable fibres (cotton, linen, jute, sisal), animal fibres (wool, silk) and man-made fibres. Each of these raw materials can be made into many different

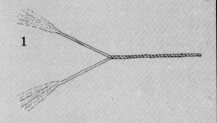

Above: Fibres are spun into singles and twisted together to make plied yarn.

Left: Yarns are packaged in different ways. From left to right are a cone, two cheeses and two hanks. The wooden spool is used for slippery yarns like silks and man-made fibres.

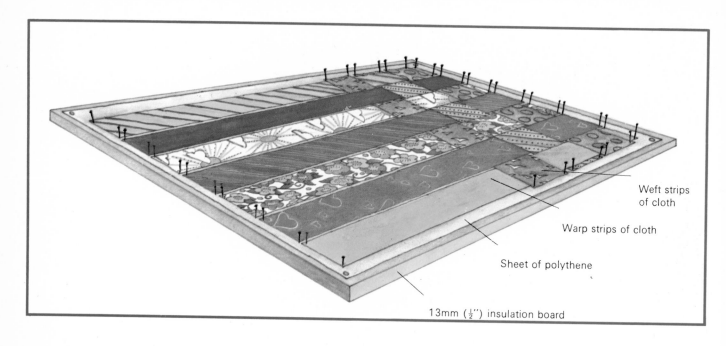

Weft strips
of cloth

Warp strips of cloth

Sheet of polythene

13mm (½″) insulation board

*Above: As well as using special
yarns for weaving, it is also
possible to weave with strips of
cloth such as cotton or rayon.*

types of thick or thin yarn, twisted tightly or softly into a smooth or
textured thread. For example, sometimes even a silk thread can be
unrecognizably dull-looking and rough because of the type of silk
fibres chosen and the way they have been spun into a thread. A
yarn, therefore, cannot be described by its fibre alone. Its behaviour
and appearance will depend not only on its fibre but also on the
way in which it has been spun into a yarn.

Properties of some fibres

Wool is a resilient fibre. There are many types of wool ranging
from soft angora to hard, rough wool suitable only for rugs. It
behaves extremely well when woven, covering spaces and forgiving
irregularities. Think how much easier it is to produce good knitting
in wool rather than in cotton. Wool is the most popular fibre for
weaving and is used as much by experienced weavers as beginners.
Linen is less easy for beginners to use as a warp because it is
affected by the moisture in the air and this makes it difficult to keep
the tension even. Two-ply linen is easier as a warp than 'singles'
which is only suitable for very experienced weavers. Linen is
hard-wearing and cold to the touch.
Cotton is easy to use, is absorbent, launders well and comes in a
good range of colours.
Silk is more suitable for experienced weavers as it needs extra care
in handling. It is also expensive and difficult to obtain.
Man-made fibres Many of these lack elasticity and need careful

Left: Strips of cloth being woven on an improvised loom made out of insulation board. The ends of the strips are secured with pins. Even a simple method such as this produces marvellous results.

handling. If possible, it is better to avoid man-made fibres until some experience has been built up in handling yarns.

Buying yarns

Some of the yarns which can be bought from wool shops are suitable for weaving, but the majority of knitting wools look 'soapy' (soft and uneven) when woven as they have a different twist to weaving wools. Knitting cottons, however, can be used, as well as fancy knitting and crochet yarns.

Hardware shops often sell a good range of strings and twines in many different fibres. Stationers stock coloured parcel and gift twines, sometimes even legal ribbons. Binder and baler twines can be obtained in agricultural areas and garden shops, and chain stores are always worth a visit. All sorts of sheet materials, plastic and cloth, are widely available, in a variety of textures and colours.

The majority of materials for weaving, however, have to be bought by post. Suppliers will send samples (some charge for these) and a price list. A minimum order of 100gram or 200gram ($\frac{1}{4}$lb or $\frac{1}{2}$lb) is usual, except for metal threads and 'specials'. Some knowledge of textile and yarn terms used is necessary in order to use the suppliers' lists effectively, so do try to learn them.

Yarn terminology

Ply does not denote thickness but the number of single strands of twisted fibres which are twisted together to make the yarn. For instance, two-ply yarn consists of two strands twisted together and may be thicker than a three-ply composed of three thinner strands.

Fold Another word for ply (two-fold).

Singles One strand only, not plied. Suitable for weaving lengths of cloth, especially tweeds, as it imbeds itself with other singles yarns to form a firm fabric. Not suitable for warp yarns or for beginners because it breaks unless handled expertly.

Count A system of numbers applied to yarns to denote thickness and, therefore, yardage per kilogram (per pound). When a stroke appears between two numbers, one of them, usually the smaller, denotes the ply of the yarn. This may be written 2/12s or 12s/2, for example, to indicate a two-ply yarn of a particular thickness. The count system varies from fibre to fibre and from region to region.

Cheviot, Harris, Welsh Types of wool fibre particularly suitable for tweeds. Harris wool is not suitable as a warp yarn or for beginners as it is too hairy. The projecting hairs catch together when weaving.

Mercerized A process which gives a permanent lustre to cotton.

Grey This refers to the natural colour of cotton and sometimes other fibres. It is not grey in colour but a soft, creamy-white.

Mohair A type of wool with long, glossy fibres which comes from the angora goat. Mohair loop yarn can be brushed after weaving to give the familiar light, fluffy finish.

Worsted A way of spinning fibres, always wool unless otherwise stated, to give a smooth yarn.

Woollen Wool fibres spun together to give a hairy yarn, unlike worsted, which is described above.

In oil Wool yarns often have a lanolin dressing to prevent them from fluffing during weaving. The lanolin is washed out after weaving, allowing the wool texture to fluff.

Cheese or spool, cone, hank or skein are various ways in which yarn is packaged. Hanks will be free from tangles on arrival, but need very careful handling. Do not remove the 'ties' until the hank is stretched out ready to be wound into a ball. Use two hands or a chair back if a skein-winder is not available. Never attempt to use yarn direct from the hank: always wind it into a ball first. Alternatively, use the sort of ball-winder which is sold for knitting machine users as a satisfactory substitute.

A cheese is meant to be supported on a horizontal rod for easy unwinding, but it can be put on a large nail hammered through a board, or held in a straight-sided jar on the floor. A cone can stand on the floor without support of any kind.

Sometimes it is possible, and more convenient, to pay just a little extra to have the yarn packaged differently from the way in which it is advertised. If it is sold in a hank, then it can be wound onto a

Window blind [shade] made from woven strips of cloth. Mats, cushions, decorative panels and many other objects can be made in the same way.

cheese or onto a cone. If sold on a cheese it can be wound onto a cone. If, for instance, it is sold in a 1.9kg (2lb) cone, it can be wound onto eight 100gram ($\frac{1}{4}$lb) cheeses.

Sett No yarn, no matter how suitable for its purpose, will give a good result unless the right spacing is chosen for the warp threads. Sett is the term used for the number of warp ends per 2.5cm (1in). A useful guide is to wind the warp yarn carefully around a ruler, making sure that the threads lie comfortably touching, side by side. Count them over 2.5cm (1in). Two-thirds of that number of threads is approximately the right sett for that yarn, depending on the weave to be used. This is the general rule for normal weaving, but it does not apply to tapestry weaving or rugs. Some yarns are not suitable for use in the warp. If in doubt, the supplier will usually advise you which to choose.

Window blind

This decorative window blind [shade] is woven with strips of cloth and reinforced with PVA adhesive.

Stretch the polythene sheeting over the insulation board and secure with pins. Using lightweight fabrics such as cottons, viscose or acetate rayons (but not wool, velvet or other man-made fibres) cut or tear strips of up to 8cm (3in) wide and the same length as the board. If thin enough fabrics are used, the blind [shade] can be mounted on a roller kit, but refer to the instructions with the kit to check size of the woven fabric required for your window.

Pin out the strips of cloth on the board side by side, with no gaps. When enough strips have been pinned out for the required width, cut or tear more strips for the weft. Darn each weft strip in and out of the warp strips, keeping them flat and pinned taut at each end. When the weaving is complete, make a solution of PVA and water. Slowly add 2/3 water to 1/3 PVA, whisking together all the time to blend thoroughly. Apply this solution liberally to the weaving with a piece of plastic sponge (if this is rinsed out immediately in cold water it will not become stiff). Although the solution looks like milk when applied, it will dry clear and transparent.

When the weaving is saturated, take some kitchen paper towelling (preferably white) and mop up as much excess moisture as possible. Leave to dry flat. If it has to be dried vertically, make sure that the floor is protected. When completely dry, the fabric can be carefully peeled off the polythene-covered board and can be trimmed to size without fear of fraying at the ends.

Some fabrics become translucent with this process and some will darken. It is wise to test small pieces first if discolouration is likely to be a disadvantage in the finished blind [shade].

Window blind

You will need :
12mm ($\frac{1}{2}$in) thick insulation board slightly larger than the finished blind is to be (available from builders' merchants).
Polythene sheeting to cover the board.
Cotton or rayon fabric.
Pins.
Plastic sponge.
PVA adhesive. PVA is obtainable from hardware shops and should be bought in a plastic container.
If it comes in a tin it tends to oxidize and can discolour the cloth.

Making a frame loom

The deceptively simple frame loom is much used by professional weavers of tapestry and sculptural weaving. The advantage of a frame, whether small or large, is that it is cheap and simple to construct, simple to set up and operate and gives great freedom in the variety of materials and shapes that can be woven.

More sophisticated looms were developed simply to fill the need for quicker and greater production of lengths of cloth. Essentially the frame loom is for the one-off piece such as a hanging or a tapestry, though of course the fabric you produce on a frame can be used for all sorts of other things. The great advantage of the frame loom is that it offers scope for endless variation and experiment with texture, colour and materials, so that the process of weaving is an exciting and satisfying end in itself.

Although frames such as picture frames may be used, they are not usually strong enough to withstand the tension from the warp without some form of modification. As frames are so simple to construct, it is a better idea to build one for the purpose than trying to make do with something you may have lying around.

The frame loom given measures 60cm by 105cm (2ft by 3ft 6 in). Although a smaller frame than this can be used, it would severely limit the size of any weaving as you have to allow 10cm (4in) in the width and 23cm (9in) in the length for wastage. The tapestry sampler in the next chapter needs a frame of this size.

Put frame together as in fig.1, using two screws per corner on each side of the frame. On one side the screws should be placed at top left and bottom right, and on the reverse of the frame at top right and bottom left. This is to prevent the screws coinciding.

In the centre, between the cross pieces at the top and bottom, insert the small blocks and screw in position. These act as spacers to prevent bending under the warp tension (fig.2).

Starting 5cm (2in) from one inside edge of the frame, mark off cross pieces A and B (fig.3) into 12mm ($\frac{1}{2}$in) intervals (making 33 along each edge), and using small nails or 3cm ($1\frac{1}{4}$in) panel pins, knock into the cross pieces on the marks at an angle (fig.4). The top and bottom nails should be exactly in line with each other. Stagger

---

Frame loom

You will need:
Two pieces of pinewood
105cm by 5cm by 2.5cm thick
(3ft 6in by 2in by 1in thick).
Four pieces of pinewood,
60cm by 5cm by 2.5cm thick
(2ft by 2in by 1in thick).
Two blocks of pinewood
5cm by 2.5cm by 8cm (2in by 1in by 3in).
Two pieces of pinewood,
6mm by 18mm ($\frac{1}{4}$in by $\frac{3}{4}$in), 70cm (28in) long, for cross sticks.
20 by 4cm ($1\frac{1}{2}$in) No. 8 screws.
66 by 3cm ($1\frac{1}{4}$in) small nails.
Cotton warp yarn, count 6/9s.

Right: The frame loom warped up ready for weaving.

The illustrations opposite show how to assemble a frame loom.
1. Putting the frame together
2. Insert the small spacer block between the two cross pieces
3. Stagger the nails to prevent the wood from splitting.
4. Side view of the frame showing the correct angle of the nails.

the nails as this helps to prevent the wood splitting and stops you catching your fingers in the nails when putting on the warp (fig. 3). **To set up the loom** Place the frame on a table or chair and lean it against a wall. It may be helpful to lay the frame on its side, as warping (putting on the warp threads) is usually easier from side to side rather than up and down.

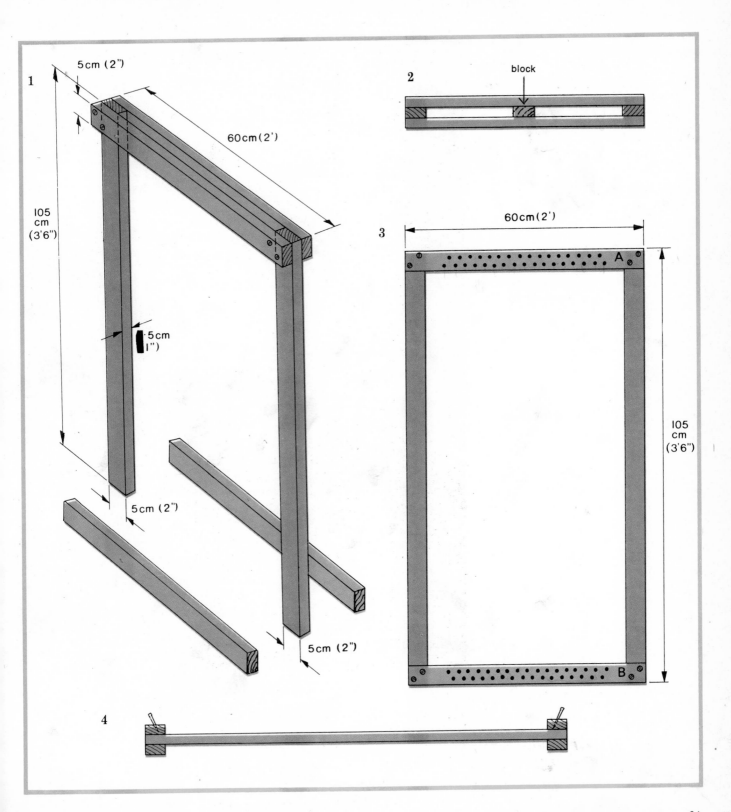

1

5cm (2")

60cm (2')

105 cm (3'6")

5cm (1")

5cm (2")

5cm (2")

2

block

3

60cm (2')

A

B

105 cm (3'6")

4

*Right: Warping up the frame.
Use two threads together, taking
them once around each nail.
Keep an even tension.*

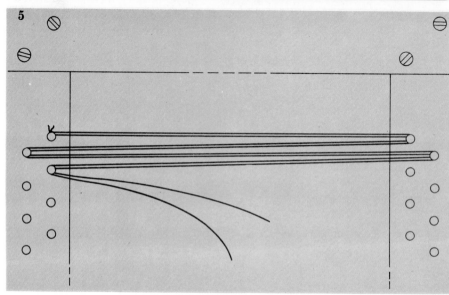

*5. Putting the warp on the
frame. The first two threads form
the selvedge.*

The following instructions refer to putting the warp on the frame while it is on its side, as shown in the picture opposite.

Wind off half of your spool of cotton thread either onto an empty spool or into a ball. Take the thread from each spool and use them together as a double thread for your warp.

Tie the cotton warp thread to the first nail at the top of the frame on the left hand side (fig.5). Holding the threads reasonably tightly, carry them across to right hand side. Pass them around first nail at the top on the right hand side. Carry them to second nail on left. Loop the threads around the left nail and carry them over to second nail on the right. Pass the threads around it and across to the third nail on the left. Now carry the threads over to the third nail on the right.

This establishes your sequence.

Continue this process downwards, looping the threads once around each nail and maintaining the same tension on the warp threads. When you come to the last nail, secure with a temporary knot. The first two extra threads at beginning and end form the selvedge with two threads together.

Sett You now have a sett of eight ends per 2.5cm (1in) (fig.6). In tapestry the average spacing between the warp ends is between four and 12 ends per 2.5cm (1in), a standard spacing.

Correcting the tension Invariably, there is an unevenness in the tension of the warp after you have finished and this can be corrected. It is worth taking the trouble to get an even tension over the warp to prevent difficulties occurring when weaving.

The tension can be corrected by working the slack along the warp from the tight side to the loose side. This is done by pulling on each warp end on the side of the nail nearer the slack (fig.7).

If your warp is really slack you should cut off the excess which has been worked around, and re-tie it as near as possible to the nail which is situated at the top of the frame.

Inserting cross sticks After adjusting the warp tension the two cross sticks are inserted. The sticks maintain the order of the threads right across the warp and make it easier to weave. They also make a useful barrier against which to weave. The two sticks are inserted near the nails at the bottom of the frame.

Take the first stick and place the first two threads of the selvedge on top of it. It does not matter which side you start from. The next warp goes under the stick, the next over, and so on across the warp. The odd warp ends are now all on top of the stick and the evens underneath. You can see this clearly in fig.8.

The second stick is inserted with the odds and evens reversed and the threads form a cross between the two sticks.

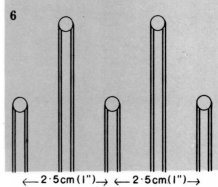

←—2·5cm(1")—→ ←—2·5cm(1")—→

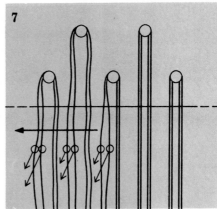

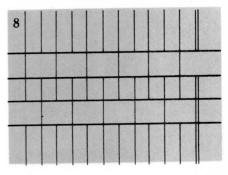

6. *Sett of eight ends per 2.5cm (1in).*
7. *Correcting the tension of the warp.*
8. *The cross sticks in the warp.*

A tapestry sampler

There are various tapestry techniques which are used to create the definition between colour and image. The sampler shown incorporates the basic shapes – lines, diagonals, circles, diamonds – which you will need when creating your own designs. Even the most elaborate medieval pictorial tapestries used these basic methods to create their intricate images and textures.

For clarity, only the two 'colours' of black and white are used, but a different range of colourways can transform a design into something entirely different in mood from this example.

Making a cartoon

Before starting to weave a tapestry it is often advisable to work out the design on paper. Many weavers find it helpful to make the paper design the same size as the final tapestry and to hang it behind the warp threads of the loom as a pattern from which to weave. This sort of accurate pattern is known as a cartoon.

Mark off the paper into 2.5cm (1in) squares. Each of the squares on your paper is represented by a square in fig.1. Using the felt pen or the adhesive paper, black in the relevant squares. Pin this behind your frame loom so that you have an outline to follow.

From the bottom to the top, the sampler is marked into sections.

Tapestry sampler

An elegant wall hanging, 71.5cm by 41cm (28½in by 16in) which combines most basic tapestry shapes.

Preparing the weft Wind some of the black weft yarn tightly around a tapestry bobbin (fig.2). Be careful not to overfill the bobbin – apart from the difficulty in passing it through the warp, there is also the danger of the yarn slipping off. Alternatively, the yarn may be wound into a tight lozenge shape instead of onto a bobbin (fig.3). Either method is suitable.

Section One

The first section of the tapestry is a solid 18mm (¾in) band of black. This section not only gives you a chance to practise weaving, but

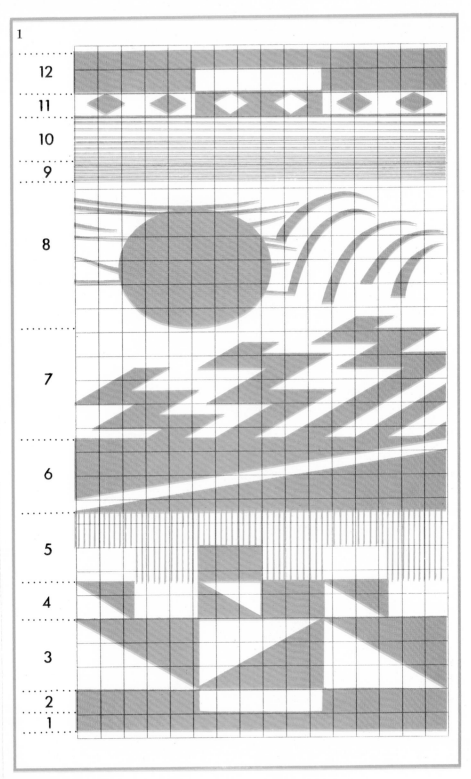

1. The pattern for the tapestry sampler. Each small square equals 2.5cm square (1 sq in) when making a full-size cartoon to hang behind the loom.
2. Bobbin wound with yarn
3. The yarn can also be wound in a lozenge shape.

Right: Pick up alternate warp ends and thrust your hand into the shed to hold the two sets of threads apart.

4a,b,c. Leave a loop of weft and beat it down with the bobbin.

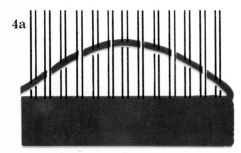

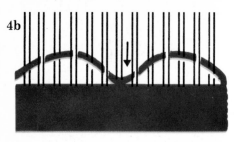

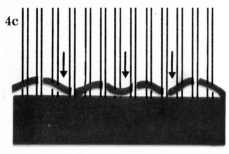

the rows of plain weave also serve to space the warp threads evenly.
Weaving from right to left To start off your weaving, hold the bobbin in the right hand and use the left hand to 'make a shed' (to lift alternate warp ends so that the bobbin can be passed behind).
To make the shed Start about 5cm (2in) in from the right selvedge and work back to the selvedge picking up the alternate threads with the thumb and first finger of the left hand. The two threads at the end should be treated as one as they form the selvedge.
By thrusting the left hand into the horizontal position behind these threads, a space (the shed) can be made between those warp ends in front of the hand and those behind. Pass the bobbin through the space created and from the right hand to the left. Keep the bobbin vertical to prevent too much weft from winding off. Continue this process by weaving small sections until the left hand side is reached.
Tension When the weft has been passed through, do not pull it tight, but form a small loop (fig.4a). It is important to leave this small loop before beating down, as a tightly pulled weft will result in the edges of the tapestry moving inwards as well as making it difficult to cover the warp properly.
On the other hand, if you leave too big a loop the width of the warp will begin to increase and loops will stick out from the face of the weaving. The correct amount of slack will be achieved with practice, as long as you follow the instructions.
After forming the loop beat it down with the point of the bobbin (while holding the bobbin end of the weft) (figs.4b and 4c).

Left: Pass the bobbin or lozenge from one hand to the other through the shed. Pull the yarn gently through.

5. An occasional extra loop at the selvedge keeps the weaving level as you work.
6. To stop the tapestry curving in you can lace it to the sides of the frame.

Weaving from left to right Pass the weft around the two threads of the left hand selvedge. With the fingers of the right hand, lift the warp ends which lay behind the weft in the previous pick. Make the shed by thrusting the hand into a horizontal position as before, and pass the bobbin through from the left to the right hand.

Selvedges During the weaving, care must be taken to keep the selvedges firm and straight. Then after each 12mm (½in) of weaving, take the weft twice around each selvedge (fig.5). This is necessary because the weft usually beats down more closely at the selvedge and this adjusts the level.

If any difficulty is experienced in preventing the edges of the tapestry from moving inwards, they can be kept straight by lacing the selvedges to the side of the weaving frame (fig.6).

Joining threads When the weft yarn which is wound around the bobbin comes to an end, the last 5cm (2in) are left hanging down either at the front or the back of the tapestry. The beginning of the next length of weft is started next to the end of the last length, again leaving 5cm (2in) hanging on the same side.

Traditionally, tapestries were woven back to front with all the ends hanging down the side facing the weaver. However, these ends tend to obscure what is happening and you may find it easier to work with the front facing you. There is no need to overlap the beginnings and ends of the weft, as tapestry weave is very firm and the ends will not pull out of the main fabric.

Beating After weaving the 18mm (¾in) of black, the weft must be

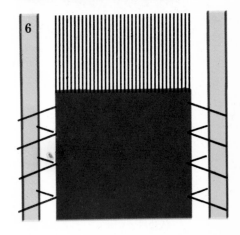

beaten down more closely. Use a heavy forked tapestry beater to do this (fig.7). They are available in crafts stores.

Tapestry weave

The aim of the conventional tapestry weave is to cover the warp fully and compactly with the weft. Unlike most other weaves where the warp and weft bend around each other, tapestry keeps the vertical warp threads straight, with the weft bending around them to form the fabric (fig.8). The warp is completely covered and the weft alone creates the design of the finished work.

Section Two

The width of the warp is now divided into three equal parts in the design. The black weft is continued up the two outside thirds for 2.5cm (1in) and a white weft is introduced into the middle third. To create a clear-cut division between the three areas of colour you will have to join the black and white wefts in a vertical line.

Joining vertically

There are three basic methods of joining two sections of weft to make a vertical line. They are as follows:

Method 1 The simplest way of making a vertical join is to pass the coloured wefts around a single warp end (fig.9). This method soon leads to a build-up of weft around the common warp and consequent bulge in the surface of the weaving.

Method 2 Paradoxically, this build-up can be decreased if alternate groups of three weft picks (rows) are looped around the same warp end (fig.10). The subsequent beating down will dovetail the loops into each other in the form of a point (fig.11). However, the sawtoothed effect is increased by this method.

Method 3 A modification of this join, which is the one used in Section Two, joins the black and white wefts over three warps (fig.12). This method of joining is strong and because the join is staggered over three warp ends it can be continued for any height without fear of build-up or distortion.

To make the vertical join Starting with the left side black weft, weave up to the warp end 2 (fig.13). This is the middle end of the three around which the join will be formed.

Pass the weft around it and return to the left selvedge. Return with the black weft and go around warp end 1. Return it to the selvedge. As you can see from fig.13, it is necessary to weave both the black and white pieces alternately to make the join, and a strict order of weaving must be maintained. This process is slightly more complicated than at first glance because Section Two has two joins and

7. A heavy, forked tapestry beater can be used to beat down the weft.
8. In tapestry the weft does the work while the warp remains straight.

both must be worked together, as the white centre weft plays its part in each join. The whole width of the warp must be worked step by step as both joins must be formed at the same time.

Taking the white weft, which should start from the right hand side of the centre third, weave until end 3 is reached (fig.13). Take the white weft around end 3 and return to the other side of the white section. As the join has also to be repeated on the right-hand side, pass the white weft around warp end 5 as shown (fig.13). Return the white weft to the left-hand side and pass it around end 2. Start the black weft on the right-hand side and weave up to and around end 6. Continue this process for 2.5cm (1in), making the two joins simultaneously. Do not forget to beat down well with the point of your bobbin as you go along.

Section Three

In this section, the vertical joins between the three main sections are made as in Section Two, method 3. The triangles are woven by increasing or decreasing the number of warp ends covered by each pick to create the triangle shape.

Diagonals The angle of incline of the diagonal is controlled either

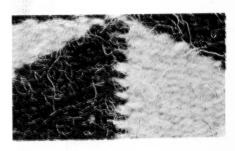

Above: Detail of vertical join and a diagonal, Section Three.

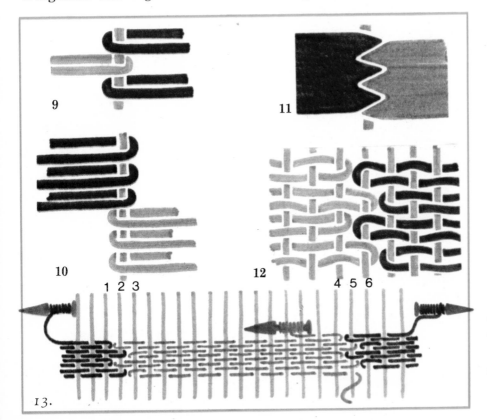

9. A simple join around one warp end.
10-11. Three threads around one warp.
12-13. Making a join around three warps.

by the number of times the weft is taken around the same warp end (fig.14) or by reducing the number of warp ends covered by the weft by one or more at a time (fig.15). The first method produces a steep incline, the second a flatter one. In Section Three, the increase and decrease is by one warp end (fig.15).

Section Four

The diagonals are woven as in the previous section, increasing and decreasing by one warp end. The method used here for weaving the vertical join is by weft interlocking. This method gives the best definition between the two colours.

Weft interlocking

Again there are three variations.

Method 1 The first is formed by interlocking the black and white weft picks between the two warp ends (fig.16). The two colours always interlock in the same direction to ensure the clearest division between the two colours. A certain amount of build-up will inevitably occur with this method.

Above: A series of steps creates a diagonal, Section Four.

14. A steep incline is produced when more than one weft is passed around each warp end.
15. A gradual incline is produced by reducing the number of warp ends covered by each weft pick.
16. First method of weft interlocking.
17. Interlocking at every other junction reduces weft build up.

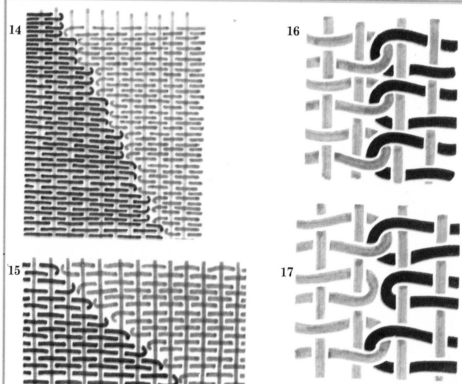

Method 2 A variation of this is the method used in the sampler. The interlocking occurs at every other junction of the two colours (fig.17). This prevents any build-up and has the added advantage of **being quick to weave, while preserving a clear division.**

Method 3 The third system of interlocking also gives a clearly defined division between the two colours (fig.18). This is slightly more complex and time consuming, but the resultant join is very solid and firm, and well worth the extra effort.

Section Five

The vertical joins between the three blocks of solid colour and the black and white stripes are made in the same way as the verticals in method 2 of Section Four. See above for method.

Vertical stripes

Weaving vertical stripes is very simple. Weave one pick with the black weft and then one pick with the white. After a few rows you will notice that the black and white wefts respectively always cover the same warp ends, thus producing the striped effect (fig. 19).

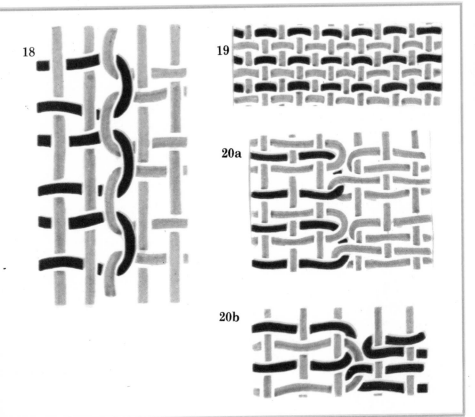

Above: Detail of stripes, Section Five.

18. *A more complex method of weft interlocking.*
19. *Forming vertical stripes.*
20a. *To make joins between stripes and blocks clearer, leave slack on the black yarn, pull white picks (P) and draw black into a loop at the back. With a straightforward join where stripes look clear (20b), no loop forming is necessary.*

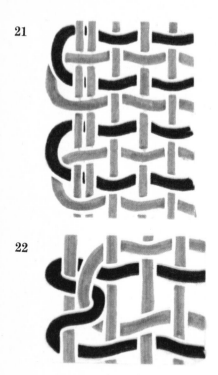

21

22

21. Locking at the selvedges.
22. An advanced technique
for selvedges.

In the first part of the section, where the stripes are between the solid colours, a little practice will be needed in order to weave neat divisions at the vertical joins (fig.20). When the top of the solid colour blocks is reached, continue the striped effect across the whole width of the warp. The impact is quite dramatic.

Selvedges

When weaving one pick of one colour followed by a pick of another colour, cross one over the other at the selvedge so that they lock (fig.21), or else the selvedge will be missed.

A neater way of forming the selvedge is to leave a loop which is pulled round the selvedge to the back of the tapestry by the other weft colour (fig.22). With this method, the crossing of the wefts is not shown and the striped effect is continued right to the edge.

Section Six

This section of diagonals is woven using the technique shown in Section Three. However, here the rate of increase is by four warp ends per pick (fig.23). This creates a gradual slope. Do not forget that the white diagonal stripe is increased on one side while at the same time being decreased on the other.

Section Seven

This area has been included for practice in weaving the shapes already explained in Sections Three and Four. The forms are more complex, and several bobbins of weft must be worked together.

In tapestry, small areas can be worked independently. It is not always necessary to build up the whole of the warp at any one time. However, you must always have woven the area directly underneath the area you are working.

Section Eight

This section is complicated as it combines several different shapes. Before you start to weave this area, read all the instructions. For clarity, the instructions for the circle have been dealt with in isolation. When you actually come to weave, you will have to combine the circle with the small black lines radiating from it.

Weaving a circle Before beginning to weave a circular shape it is advisable to mark out the shape on the warp with a broad felt-tipped pen. The curve of the circle is woven using a combination of diagonal and vertical weft joining.

Start by weaving the white background. Two separate bobbins of white will be required, one for working the left side and the other for the right. From the centre of the bottom curve, start weaving the background on one side, gradually increasing the slope by the method explained for weaving diagonals (fig.24). There will not be a regular increase as there is with diagonals and you will have to follow the outline of the circle on the warp. Remember to weave slightly higher than the outline to make up for the loss when beating down. Continue the increasing until the weft is passing three times around a single warp end. Weave the background on the other side in the same manner. The lower portion of the black circle can now be woven up to the level of the background.

From this point in weaving the circle, vertical weft joining should be used for weaving the steepest part of the circle. You can choose any of the methods described in Section Two. Both background wefts and circle weft should be built up together.

As the steepness of the slope declines (from the point where the black weft is passing three times around a single warp end), continue weaving the circle by modifying the steepness of the diagonal weave until the circle is complete.

Remember, these instructions are for weaving a circle with a plain background. As the sampler has black stripes coming out of it, these will have to be woven in as you weave the circle.

Horizontal thin stripes These come out from the circle and are woven by continuing the black weft from the circle into the background for two, and occasionally three, picks. Watching out for the stripes, weave the circle and the background, following the instructions for weaving a circle given above.

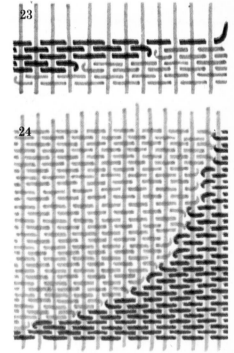

23. *Creating a gradual incline.*
24. *Forming the curve.*

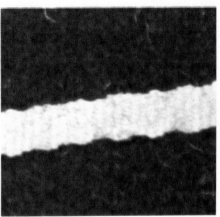

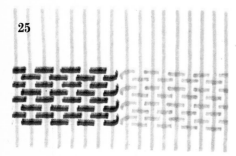

25

26

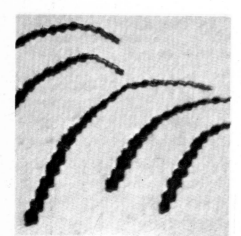

Above: Curved lines in steps.
Right: Stripes in Section Nine.
Opposite: Making the sampler.

The black curved lines on the right-hand side are formed by using the circle techniques. The steep part is woven with the weft going four times around one warp end without any interlocking. This type of join forms small slits (fig.25). In all cases where verticals are used they can be woven in this manner with the resulting slits becoming a design feature, as in Kelim rugs. Alternatively, they can be sewn up afterwards at the back.

Section Nine
The thin, slightly wavy lines are created by weaving two picks of black, followed by two picks of white and so on. To avoid unsightly loops at the selvedges, cover the weft not being used by the working weft (fig.26).

Section Ten
Weave three picks of white, one pick of black, followed by three white, one black and so on. Continue this for about 12mm (½in). Increase the number of white weft picks to five but still only weave one pick of black. Extend the blocks of white to seven and then nine picks, at regular intervals, to give a progressive shading effect from dark to light. Once again carry the black weft up the selvedge, covering it with the white as in the previous section (fig.26), until the black is required again for working.

Section Eleven
At this point, the width of the warp is again divided into three equal parts. The diamond shapes, black on white, white on black, are woven using the normal diagonal technique, and the vertical joins by method 3, Section Two.

Section Twelve
The last part of the sampler is a repeat of the first two sections. This is a 2.5cm (1in) area divided into three blocks, two black on the outsides and white in the centre, followed by 18mm (¾in) of black.

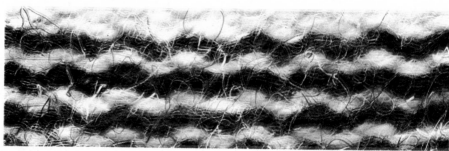

Taking tapestry off loom

Cut the warp from the frame leaving a sufficient length of warp, about 8cm (3in), to allow for tying knots. At the bottom of a tapestry this means cutting the warp as near the nails as possible. There are several ways in which the edge can be finished off. If the edge is to be turned under and sewn, then the ends of the warp can be cut much closer. The simplest method is to tie a series of overhand knots (fig.27). Make sure that you try to get the knot as close to the weaving as you possibly can.

Because tapestry is such a firm, compact weave, it is not absolutely necessary to darn in the loose weft ends. If you leave them loose trim them down to a tidy length of about 5cm (2in). Brush lightly to get rid of any loose fibres which may still be clinging to the surface of the tapestry. As it is pure wool and cotton, you can wash your tapestry gently when it gets dirty.

27

Top: Finishing off with overhand knots
Above: Leave the fringe long if you wish it to be a design feature

Right: Detail of the lower left hand corner of the tapestry.

The completed tapestry should have straight, even edges. If they are pulled in, careful stretching with an iron may help.

Designing in tapestry

By this stage you should be sufficiently familiar with all the basic tapestry shapes to enable you to work on your own designs. This can be done by modifying and combining one or more of the techniques already learned. You will find that your own designs, whether pictorial or abstract, can be broken down into straight lines, diagonals or curves in one way or another. You can draw a cartoon before you start as shown for the totebag (fig.3), or you may find it more exciting to create the design on the loom itself. Before you start weaving your own designs, you will need to have some guidelines in the selection and spacing of your yarns.

The warp

The warp should be made of a strong thread, relative to the size and heaviness of the weaving to withstand the tension and support the weight. It should also be reasonably smooth to allow the weft to be beaten down easily. The warp yarn must have some elasticity so that it can recover from the stretch imposed when making a shed. The yarn should also have a good twist as this increases strength and soft yarns with little spin are liable to fray and break during the weaving process. Two of the most suitable yarns are cotton twine and linen warp yarn, and both give excellent results.

Cotton twine is strong, elastic and easy to dye.

Linen warp yarn must have a good twist otherwise it will fray, but it is strong and its natural colour is very pleasing. It is a little more difficult to handle having little elasticity and should be avoided until some experience is gained.

The warp colour is unimportant where the warp is to be completely covered by the weft. With more experimental kinds of weaving such as weaving with unusual materials or objects, the warp may not be completely covered and would therefore need to be chosen with this factor in mind.

Warp spacing or sett The closeness of the warp threads to each other determines the thickness of the tapestry to be woven. For a

A beautiful totebag woven on a frame loom.

fine weaving with detailed and precise shapes a closely set warp is necessary. This could contain as many as 20 warp ends per 2.5cm (1in) or more. However, to weave something so fine is very time-consuming and generally results in the loss of texture and yarn qualities. In tapestry, the average spacing of the warp ends is between four and 12 ends per 2.5cm (1in).

With the frame loom made for the tapestry sampler the tacks were spaced at 12mm ($\frac{1}{2}$in) intervals and the warp for the sampler was eight ends per 2.5cm (1in). If a sett of four ends per 2.5cm (1in) is required, simply wind one warp thread around each tack with an extra thread each end to form the selvedge (fig.1).

For 12 ends per 2.5cm (1in) wind three threads around each tack.

Weft yarn

Before starting to weave, a choice of weft yarn must be made. It is always extremely interesting to experiment with yarns of differing colours, thicknesses and textures.

A rough guide to the thickness necessary in tapestry is that the weft yarn should just fill the space between two consecutive warp ends with only a slight clearance on either side. In the sampler, a warp spacing of eight ends per 2.5cm (1in) was chosen and the weft used was three-ply rug wool. As the weft thickness is dependent on the warp spacing, a spacing of four ends per 2.5cm (1in) needs a weft of twice that thickness. Conversely, a closer warp needs a finer weft.

Combining weft threads The required thickness of weft can be achieved by using several thin threads together instead of a single thick thread. When using several threads together be sure to wind them onto the bobbin with an even tension to prevent some threads becoming longer than others while weaving.

This technique can be particularly interesting when working with colour if several different colours or tone of the same colour are blended together. This can be used to create a shading effect between two dominant colours. Alternatively, you can use hatching. This is the term given to irregular lines and areas of colour, a form which was used extensively on medieval tapestries. Hatching gives an indistinct shading effect (fig.2).

General tips Try to keep your first design simple – to be over ambitious at this stage may well result in failure. Avoid long, thin, vertical lines in the design. Shapes and lines are so much easier to weave across than upwards that if a design has many upright features it should be woven sideways. Do not weave individual shapes higher than about 10cm (4in) without filling in the background and always weave slightly higher than the outline on the cartoon to allow for beating down.

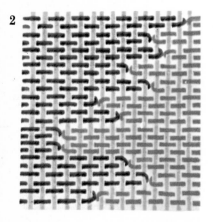

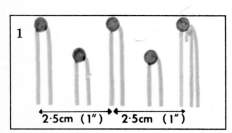

1. A sett of four ends per 2.5cm (1in) with the extra thread for the selvedge.

2. Hatching, or joining colours irregularly, produces an effective shaded pattern.

Opposite: Four variations on a landscape woven in one tapestry and showing the subtle effects that can be achieved by using closely related colours.

When weaving your own designs, begin the tapestry with a plain band of at least 18mm (¾in). This spaces the threads evenly across the warp and gives you something to turn under after the weaving has been taken off the loom. If you want your design to have a fringe without the band, you can simply pull out the first few rows after the weaving has been completed.

Keeping an even width

One of the commonest problems experienced by beginners is the gradual decreasing in the width of the tapestry. The narrowing process is so slow that it can go by unnoticed until it is too late. Keep a tape measure handy and check continually as the only remedy is to unpick and start all over again.

The cause of this fault is usually too much tension in the weft. Do not forget that the weft thread must have enough slack to go around each warp end. Always leave the loop of weft as mentioned in Section One of the sampler before beating down. If you have problems, also check that you have a thick enough weft in relation to your warp spacing this should maintain the width.

The tote bag

This is an excellent project to try after the sampler as it gives practice in weaving diagonals and curved shapes.

The weaving measures 54cm by 41cm (21½in by 16in) to make a bag 52cm by 41cm (20in by 16in).

As a sett of six ends per 2.5cm (1in) is needed, knock another set of small nails into the reverse side of the cross bars on the frame loom. They should be 8mm (⅓in) apart and staggered. It is well worth doing this, even if you do not plan to make up the totebag, as a sett of six ends per 2.5cm (1in) is a very useful alternative to four or eight ends per 2.5cm (1in) for other projects.

Warp up your frame with the cotton twine taking the warp once around every small nail and remembering the extra selvedge thread at each end. Your warp should measure about 42cm (16½in). Make a full size cartoon by copying the design (fig.3). Each square represents 2.5cm sq (1in square).

Weave 18mm (¾in) of plain tapestry weave. The colour is irrelevant as this section merely spaces the warp threads evenly and will be lost in the turning when making up the bag. The bag is woven on its side. Follow the cartoon, remembering to weave slightly above the outline to allow for beating down. The curved shapes are woven using a combination of diagonals and vertical joining as in Section Eight of the sampler. In the last section where there are vertical upright joins, weave A, B and C separately, leaving slits.

Tote bag

You will need:
A 100g (¼lb) skein in each of five different colours of 2-ply rug wool. Orange, rust, brown, cream and slate grey were used in the bag illustrated, but as some suppliers only sell non-repeatable colours in order to keep their prices down you may have to adapt your colour scheme and choose from suppliers' current stock.
Medium thickness cotton thread for the warp.
Frame loom.
Panelpins or small nails.
Upholstery needle.
Silk or synthetic sewing threads.

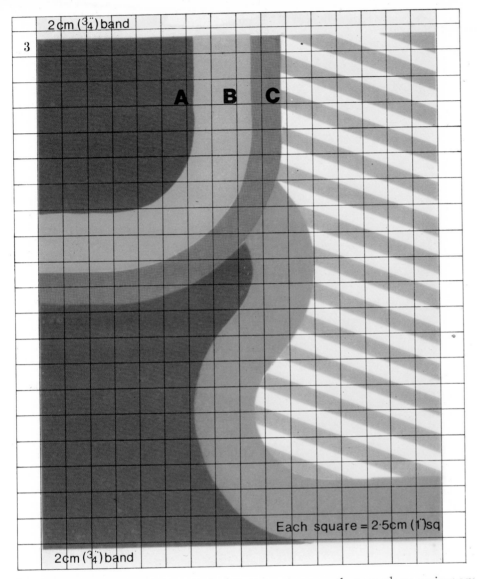

2cm (¾) band

3

A   B   C

Each square = 2·5cm (1")sq

2cm (¾) band

Draw this cartoon for the bag to full size, and hang it behind your loom as an accurate guide to your work.

As the areas build up, sew the pieces temporarily together, using an upholstery needle and a piece of contrasting yarn. Finish with 18mm (¾in) of plain tapestry weave. Cut the piece off the loom. No knotting is necessary as the weaving will be secured when sewing up the bag. Unpick the temporary stitches and sew up the slits on each side of B and C carefully using a strong, fine silk or synthetic thread. Use the tapestry as if it were a piece of material when making up the bag. Line the bag with strong cotton and use suede for the gussets at sides and bottom as well as for the back of the bag. The top suede pieces to which the handles are attached can be strengthened with a metal or wooden rod.

Variations
on texture

Effect of two rows of soumak

To relieve the flatness of a tapestry you may want to incorporate areas of textural contrast. This can be done by experimenting with fancy yarns or unusual materials or by using ordinary yarn in an unusual way. Never be frightened to experiment as there are no hard and fast rules, and you can invent your own techniques.

Here are some long established techniques to start you off.

The Ghiordes knot

The Ghiordes or Turkish knot is more commonly associated with rugs but it can give an interesting tufted effect when incorporated with tapestry, especially if you use different materials.

Loop the yarn as illustrated (fig.1) over two warp ends and pull it down to the weaving. Do not pull too tightly or you will alter the spacing of the warp threads. If you wish to get the tuft lying in the opposite direction, make the knot in the reverse way (fig.2). A row of knots can either be made separately using short pieces of yarn or several can be made with a continuous thread (fig.3). Irregular tufts can create a shingled effect especially if made with an unusual material such as thin strips of suede. Usually, however, a thick, multi-ply yarn is used so that a firm shaggy tuft is created.

Always weave at least one and preferably two rows of ordinary tapestry weave between rows of knots. Traditionally, knots are always made over the same two warp ends however many rows of knots are made on your main fabric (fig.4).

Soumak

Soumak gives a nice raised contrast to tapestry weave. It can be woven over every warp end (fig.5) or you can miss out a regular number of warp ends (fig.6). Two consecutive rows of soumak can be woven and if the direction is altered an interesting plaited [braided] effect, like knitting stitches, is created (fig.7). Strengthen your weaving with a pick of tapestry weave between rows of soumak.

Twining

Another technique is to twist two weft threads between the warp

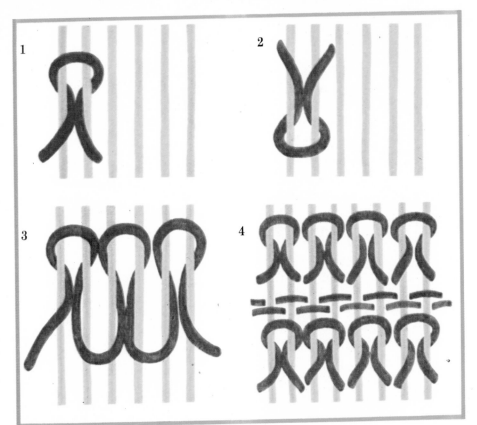

1. The Ghiordes knot creates a tufted effect.
2. An upward knot.
3. Knots are made with one thread.
4. Strengthen the knots with rows of weaving.

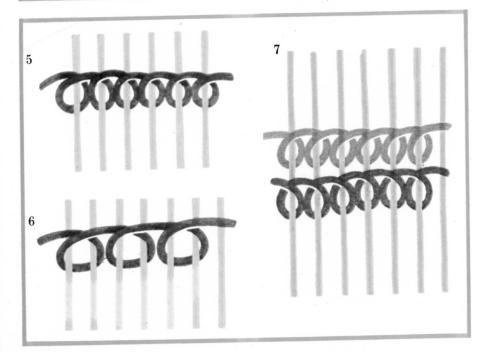

5. Soumak makes a raised area.
6. Missing out warp ends
7. Rows in different colours

ends (fig.8). Again, you can miss out warp threads (fig.9) or do two rows together, alternating the coloured wefts (fig.10).

Stripes

Bands of plain colour which cover the whole width of the warp can be woven quickly if the process of making a shed is mechanically operated. To do this you need two additions to your loom – a thin piece of wood to lift the even threads up and a system of leashes or heddles to lift the odd warp ends.

Shed stick

A piece of pinewood 12mm by 4cm by 61cm ($\frac{1}{2}$in by 1$\frac{1}{2}$in by 24in) should be inserted near the top of the frame under the even warp ends and over the odd ones, just like a row of weaving. When the shed stick is stood on its side it lifts the even warps and the bobbin can be passed straight through the shed completing one pick of weaving. This speeds your weaving process.

Leashes

There are two methods of leashes suitable for the small frame loom: **Simple method** Cut lengths of cotton yarn 38cm (15in) long. You will need enough cotton lengths to lift up half of the number of warp ends in your frame. Pass each cotton length around an odd warp end below the shed stick. Gather them together into groups of six. Tie them together in groups of six so that the knot is about 6cm (2$\frac{1}{2}$in) above the warp (fig.11).

With this method the number of warp ends lifted at a time is six and each row has to be woven in small chunks. This method is useful for small areas of solid colour but the leashes have a tendency to slide down and obstruct the weaving.

Advanced method A more satisfactory way of dealing with leashes is to tie them onto a rod which is placed across the warp. Screw the two clamps to the outside of the frame loom uprights, about one third of the way down from the top. Tie the rod securely to the G-clamps [C-clamps]

Push the two cross sticks up the warp so that they lie about 2.5cm (1in) below the dowel rod. Tie them to the sides of the frame. The cross sticks ensure that the leashes will all be of the same length as they keep the warp threads even.

Cut the cotton yarn into 38cm (15in) lengths. You will need enough lengths to cover every other warp thread. Pick up an odd warp end from between the cross sticks and pass a leash around it (fig.12). Tie the leash to the dowel rod with a reef knot. Repeat this with all the other odd warp ends. The leashes should all have

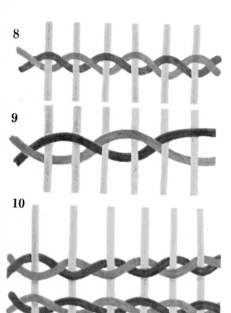

8,9,10. *Twining is another technique that gives textural interest to tapestry. Missing out warp ends or using two different colours are interesting variations.*

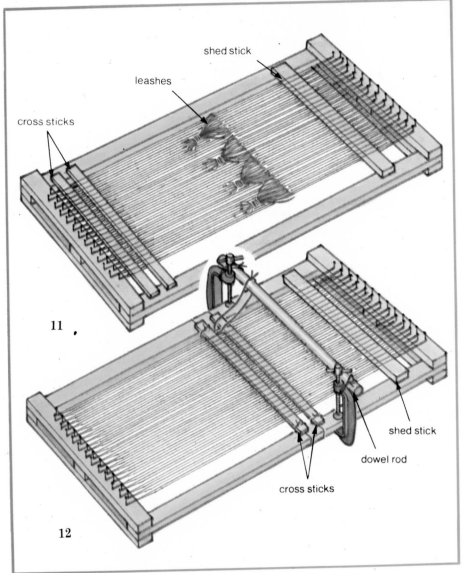

shed stick

leashes

cross sticks

11

12

shed stick

dowel rod

cross sticks

Advanced leashes

You will need:
Two 10cm **(4in)** G-clamps
[C-clamps].
Dowel rod, 61cm (24in) long and
2.5cm (1in) in diameter.
Cotton yarn.
Frame loom.

11. *Simple method of putting
leashes on the frame loom.*
12. *Tying leashes round a dowel
rod using the cross sticks to keep
them even.*

the same amount of slack. Untie the cross sticks and return them
to their normal position on the frame.

Weaving with leashes

To weave a horizontal stripe or solid area of colour, all you have to
do is pass the shuttle through the sheds made first by standing the
shed stick on its side and then by pulling on the leashes. The shed
stick will lift all the even threads and after the stick has been
returned to its horizontal position, the leashes will automatically
lift the odd warp ends as you pull them.

The cushion cover

The cushion cover uses all of the techniques described already. The striped flat area in the middle is 30cm (12in) square and was woven using leashes for speed. The textural area at either end of the cover includes soumak, twining and Ghiordes knots. The final cushion cover measures 30cm by 45cm (12in by 18in).

Warp up 31cm (12½in) of your frame loom so that you have a sett of eight ends per 2.5cm (1in). Put leashes on using either method described above. As you will be weaving 30cm (12in) of tapestry going from selvedge to selvedge it is probably advisable to adopt the advanced method using G-clamps [C-clamps].

Weave about 12mm (½in) with any waste yarn you have available. This area of weaving simply brings the threads together and spaces them easily – it will be pulled out after the cushion cover is finished. It also gives you a nice straight edge for the real first row of the cushion cover. Choose any colour wool and weave about 6mm (¼in). Although this area will be part of the final cover, it will be covered by the overhanging tufts.

Cut 15cm (6in) lengths of two colours of six-ply rug wool (alternatively use three-ply doubled). Miss out the double thread of the selvedge and using alternate colours make a row of downward Ghiordes knots on each pair of warp threads (see fig.1).

Take your weft thread from the previous area of weaving and wrap it twice around the selvedge so that it is covered. (You can of course change the colour, but do remember to bind the selvedges.) When you get to the other side bind that selvedge. Weave two picks of tapestry weave in three-ply wool.

Do a row of knots using 12.5cm (5in) lengths of yarn. Make the knots around the same warp ends as were used in the previous row and keep to the same colour scheme to achieve the striped effect. Weave two picks of tapestry weave in the three-ply wool.

Do a row of knots using 10cm (4in) lengths. Do not forget to wrap around the selvedges ot each row of knots. Weave a few rows of plain tapestry weave in three-ply until your weaving measures 2.5cm (1in) from the top of the waste yarn (ie the beginning of the weaving proper). Now you can begin your contrast.

Do two consecutive rows of soumak using only one colour six-ply yarn. Go over four and back two warp ends as in fig.6 and reverse the direction of the rows to achieve braided effect (fig.7). Weave a pick of plain tapestry weave with three-ply yarn. Weave two more rows of soumak using a different colour yarn. Weave 6mm (¼in) of plain tapestry weave. Do two rows of twining using two colours of six-ply yarn in each row to achieve the braided effect (see fig.10). Weave two picks of plain tapestry weave. Do two more rows of

Opposite: The finished cushion cover looks very attractive.

59

Above: Detail of the textured area of the cushion cover showing the final effect of knots, soumak and twining.
Right: Pull the leashes to lift the odd warps. The shed stick lifts the evens.

twining. This should bring you up to about 8cm (3in) from the top of the waste yarn where the weaving begins.

Using the leashes, weave plain bands of colour for the next 30cm (12in). Either make regular stripes or avoid all pattern making by going for irregular areas of contrast. Use as many colours as you like. After you have completed 30cm (12in) of the striped area, you simply repeat the first 8cm (3in) only in reverse. The knots should be made upwards (see fig.2) so that they fall in the opposite direction to the ones at the other end. There is no need to weave the area of waste yarn at the end of the work.

Finishing off Cut the piece off the loom and cut the warp loops. Unpick the area of waste yarn. Using a darning needle, thread each warp end up inside the back of the weaving. This creates a nice clean straight edge at each end. Fray out the tufts of the knots so that they have a nice velvety effect. Trim them if you prefer them shorter or less regular. Make up into a cushion cover with a contrasting, plain material as the reverse side.

Wrapping techniques

The technique of wrapping is very simple and requires no tools or mechanical aids other than yarn and a pair of scissors, yet its range of application is vast. Single strands of wrapping can be used to create such objects as necklaces and belts; it is a very useful method of adding textural interest or finishing off a hanging; it can even be the method of construction for entire wall hangings. Whatever way you choose to use it, wrapping is great fun.

Wrapping is taught in boy scout and girl guide [girl-scout] trainings and may be familiar to many readers as a merely functional form of whipping. Historically, it was probably used originally for its purely practical benefits – as knife or axe handle surfaces, the hand-grip on bows or for securing rope splices. Its decorative uses are fairly widespread in the finishing of warp ends and the making of tassels and some ancient Peruvian textiles used wrapping to outline the warp threads in patterns before they were woven with a one-colour weft. The method has been used all over the world.

Contemporary applications

Today wrapping is used in many different crafts and in widely varying contexts as might be expected of a technique so simple to apply. It is used in conjunction with metal, wood, plastic and leather, although its most common application is with yarn in a weaving context. Besides its decorative application, wrapping can be used to strengthen a soft or fragile element almost to the point of rigidity if needs be or to disguise and secure a knot or join.

Wrapping on its own Perhaps its most exciting application is to be seen when wrapping is used on its own. The tough, tubular appearance of a wrapped section of a hanging provides a stark contrast to the full, soft texture of an area fully unwrapped, especially if the 'core' material itself is interesting.

How to wrap

Separate strands of wrapped yarn can be made into handsome necklaces or belts. For wrapping materials, it is normal to use cotton, linen, string or synthetic yarns as these have more tensile

Right: A multitude of wrapped tassels in a beautiful hanging.

1-4. To wrap, lay end A along the area to be wrapped. Wrap with end B. Thread B through the loop and pull end A until B disappears.

strength than wool which is inclined to break when being pulled through the wraps in the last stage of the operation. In this context, wool provides a very pleasant 'core' rather than a surface.

For the necklaces, use thin linen warp for the core and fine rayon for the silky wraps. Lay one end of the wrapping element (A in fig.1), along the length of the core element (X). The other end of the wrapping element (B) is then brought back in a loop to the point where the wrapping is to begin. Keeping the loop in position, lay end B in tight consecutive wraps for as much of the area as needs to be covered (fig.2). Thread the end B through the remains of the loop at the bottom of the wrapping. Pull on end A until end B disappears under the wraps (fig.3). Trim off end A (fig.4).

Easy weft wrapping

Interesting effects can be achieved by the controlled wrappings of elements such as braiding which can be woven in like weft with perhaps one end hanging freely on the surface of the weaving.

When used as weft, wrapped elements can be as skinny or as chunky as you like depending on the effect you wish to create.

Warp wrapping

Individual warps or groups of warps can also be wrapped in a tapestry context. This can be used, as in some old Peruvian weaves, as a method of outlining a geometric image (fig.5).

Warp wrapping is useful where a more open effect is wanted in a weave. In this case where adjacent threads are wrapped, wrap the warp threads together in groups to prevent the weave from slipping up and down as shown in fig.6.

If eight to 12 adjacent wrap threads of identical lengths are treated this way, and the weft discontinued for that area, then a small window of vertical bars is created in a weave (fig.6).

Wrapped fringes

Wrapping the end warp threads can be done where warp fringing would look unsatisfactory, ie a dark toned hanging with a white cotton warp. Gather the warp threads into groups and wrap from the very edge of the weaving (fig.7).

If a very long, decorative fringe is desired, start your weaving high up on the frame. Then wrap the empty bottom warp threads when the weaving section has been completed. It is much easier to leave the warp threads attached to the frame when wrapping long sections as they are fixed in a stable position. Where long sections are to be wrapped, the loop can be dispensed with until the very end. The first end can be caught and covered by the wraps.

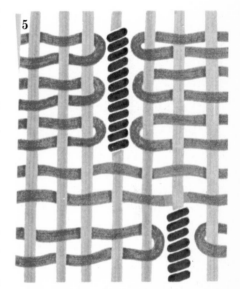

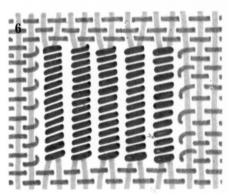

5. *Wrapping individual warp ends*
6. *Window of wrapping warps.*

7. Wrapping to finish
off a weaving.

Right: Colourful weaving with
intricate warp wrapping and
thick wrapped tassels in silk.

If you have a very large frame then a door curtain could be constructed in this way by weaving a small strip at the top of the frame wrapping the warp threads in groups.

Including beads

If you want to hang objects such as beads on your wrapped threads, cut the warp threads before wrapping and thread on all the required beads. Retie the warp threads to the frame and wrap the warp threads positioning the beads where you want them. Wrap down to the bead, thread the wrapping element through the hole of the bead and continue wrapping. Make sure that the hole of the bead is big enough for both the warp and wrapping threads.

Wrapped tassels

One of the most obvious applications of wrapping is the wrapped tassel. After reaching proportions of epic grandeur in Victorian times, the tassel suffered a sad decline until more recent years. Now our slowly returning sense of tactile opulence permits the more lavish use of such decorations.

A single tassel can be a lovely object, the cut ends providing an almost furry contrast to the smooth, wrapped stem which can be given added brilliance by wrapping with contrasting colours.

Where a mass of tassels is used together to decorate a surface, the effect is baroque in its richness.

To make tassels Gather the warp threads into groups. Wrap as in fig.7 and described above. Take a group of yarns of equal length and double over the middle. Knot into position with two warp ends (fig.8). Tuck the extra warps into the centre of the tassel. Wrap tassel to cover over the knot (fig.9).

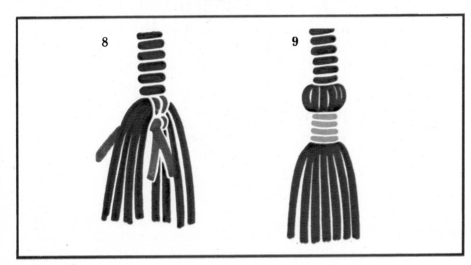

8,9. Wrapped tassels can add rich texture and an unusual dimension to a weaving.

Adding new materials

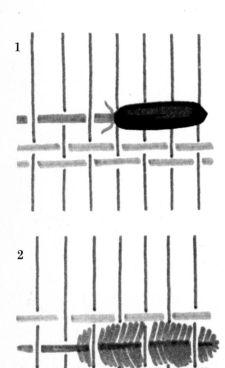

1. Stem of bulbous object woven
into the warp.
2. Fragile object caught
in the warp.

Opposite: Fragile objects such as
dried grasses can create a
delicate effect. This weaving
was made on a table loom
with varied spacing in the warp.

Weaving is a visual, tactile and involving experience and there are many materials apart from yarn which you can use as either the basic inspiration for a piece of weaving or as an addition to it. Materials such as beads, feathers and ribbons can often contribute much to the visual presence of a piece of work. You can use such objects for their colour, texture, or contour.

Sometimes found objects can quite accidentally be the solution to a design problem. In one weaving for example, the warp threads at the bottom, which already had feathers hanging from them, needed some sort of extra weight. Fishermen's lead weights were ideal and added just the right visual effect. Unusual materials can add a whole new dimension to weaving tapestry on a frame loom.

Magpie materials

The frame loom allows the weaver great freedom in the use of objects and materials either as textural weft or as free-hanging elements. Quite ordinary things can be incorporated in tapestry to create extraordinary effects. Use materials that relate to your surroundings such as metal washers, synthetic fibres, wire, metal rods; shells, rope washed ashore, rushes; dyed stocking, raffia, netting, sequin waste or scraps of fur.

Wrap warp threads with balls of tinsel, colourfully striped garden string or metallic glitter threads. Hang objects from your weaving such as small toys, tassels, bells, shapes of glass or plastic, or anything else that catches your eye.

Dried plant material

When using anything as fragile as dried flowers or leaves, their condition and durability are important factors. To be quite sure that they are not going to crumble, either spray them before weaving with a clear spray, such as hair lacquer, or brush a clear glue on to flat objects such as leaves. You can buy already treated material or dry the leaves and flowers yourself.

Thick stems Beware of stems or twigs that are too thick for your weaving as they can change and disrupt the tension of your warp

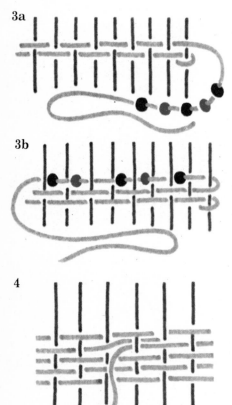

threads. If you must use them, try to have them at the end of your work near the top of the loom.

Weaving in dried objects Weave up to where you want the leaf to be positioned. If the object is flat (or will lie flat as will skeleton leaves or dried flowers), lay it in the open shed. Either place your weft in with the object or weave around it using a bobbin.

Be very gentle especially when beating down. Between rows of objects always have at least two rows of plain weave to strengthen and secure the weaving. You can use objects when weaving on a table loom as well as in tapestry. Table looms are dealt with in a later chapter but the same rules apply.

Quite hairy or bulbous objects work well in a heavy weaving. Weave in the stem, leaving the textural element on the surface (fig.1). Flat objects can be woven in (fig.2) and work well in a quite open, light weave with possibly a thin linen warp and weft. Always be very gentle when weaving around fragile objects.

Beads

There are so many to choose from: antique ones, wooden, glass, Venetian, plastic, ceramic, papier maché, shaped hearts, stars, fruit, teardrops, birds and many more. The only problem with beads is that their holes are usually not very large. If you are weaving beads in with your weft thread, the hole has to be large enough to thread a needle and yarn through. When weaving them in just thread them onto the weft thread (fig.3a) and position them where you want between the warp threads (fig.3b). Alternatively, you can hang them from a weft thread with a knot at the end of the bead and start a new area of weft (fig.4).

Free-hanging beads Beads are most beautiful when hanging freely from warp threads with wrapping or threaded onto the fringe (figs.5 and 6). After your weaving is finished and you are using beads with long areas of wrapping, always be sure to cut the warp threads you are using and thread the beads through before retying the warp threads to start wrapping. As a fantasy touch, beads may also, of course, be sewn on the hanging after the weaving is finished.

Suede and chamois

Unused pieces of chamois leather and suede can sometimes be bought from leather goods manufacturers. Chamois is ideal but suede is just as useful if it is soft and pliable. Cut the suede or chamois into strips of varying widths and lengths and use the strips like a piece of yarn. Those warps which are missed out in one row should be covered in the next to keep your weaving firm. You can also use suede and chamois for making the soumak stitch

3a,b. Beads threaded on weft
4. Bead hung from weft thread

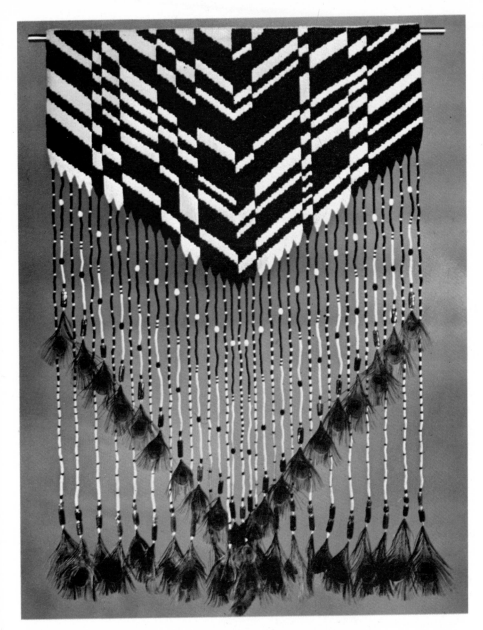

Left: The long warp ends of this
stark, geometric tapestry are
wrapped, threaded with beads and
decorated with peacock feathers.

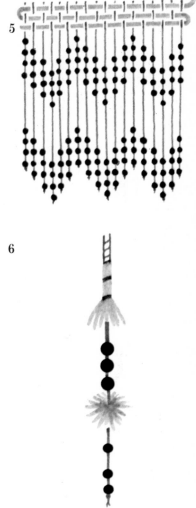

or the Ghiordes knot. Thick suede can be woven in a straight strip
without pressing or beating down too much. It looks good with a
coloured warp and the suede has a beautiful matt finish.

Try not to make two successive rows of loops or knots as they will
not hold properly. Always weave at least two rows of plain weave
before making another row of knots to strengthen the fabric. It is
also fun to scissor cut bits of coloured suede in circles and thread
them with beads onto hanging warp ends.

5. Beads hanging on warp ends
6. Wrapped warp with beads

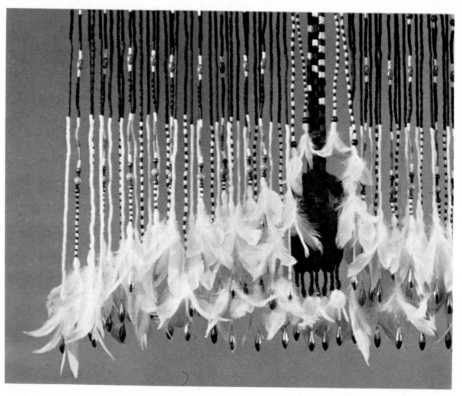

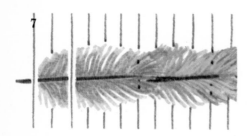

Above: Overlapping feathers
Right: Richly decorated warp
ends in a tapestry.

Feathers

Local butchers can often help by keeping you supplied with plumage from domestic and game fowl – polka-dotted guinea fowl feathers, shimmery gold and red-brown pheasant feathers or sturdy wing and tail feathers of turkeys and geese. Feathers can also be collected in the country. Failing that, feather dusters can be artificially recycled. Shops that sell fishing tackle have beautiful feathers but they are expensive.

Weaving in feathers is a slow process, but if you can build up an area weaving in feathers it is worth the time and patience. Make sure the feathers are long enough – neck feathers are wonderfully colourful but much too short for weaving. If the feather has a thick shaft, hammer it flat first. If the shaft does not need hammering, use your fingers to take the stiffness out. Weave in all of the shaft and overlap with the next feather (fig. 7). Between each row of feathers, remember to weave in ordinary weft to strengthen the fabric.

Wrapping feathers Feathers are also very effective at the end of a wrapped thread. You must have a long enough shaft and feather to wrap it securely so that it will not slip out. If it is a long feather, like a peacock's, you must hammer the rather three-sided shaft flat and cut it to about 10cm (4in) long before wrapping around it.

Beginning tablet weaving

In Europe, the earliest existing fragments of tablet weave date from the Bronze Age. This ancient craft is a form of warp twined weaving, a method of textile construction that has been practised for many hundreds of years and the origins of which were probably in rope making. It is a fascinating method to learn.

Off the loom

No loom or frame is necessary for tablet weaving as the threads may be tied between any two supports such as a door knob and the arm of an upright chair. To keep the warp threads in sequence, they are threaded through holes in square cards. By turning the cards or tablets the different coloured threads are twisted together and a different shed is made by this basic process.

With this method of weaving, beautifully patterned braids may be created which can be made into belts, ties, chokers, necklaces and straps or used as decorative trimmings and edges. Only narrow fabrics can be produced but several lengths can be joined together with a flat stitch to make into shoulder bags, cushion covers or even rugs. The possibilities are really infinite.

Basic techniques

If you take four threads and turn them several times in one direction, they twist around each other and form a spiral rope-like structure (fig.1). This is the basic technique.

Tablet weaving consists of a number of such ropes, running lengthwise parallel to each other and connected one to the other by the weft thread weaving to and fro (fig.2). Each tablet holds four threads and is responsible for one four-ply rope. The tablets act as a loom and hold the threads in order. They are the means by which the threads are twisted into ropes and enable a number of ropes to be made simultaneously thus producing a fabric.

The yarn is threaded through the holes in the tablets and weaving proceeds. Because of the position of the holes, the threads naturally separate into two layers – an upper and a lower layer – forming a shed and allowing the weft thread to pass easily between them.

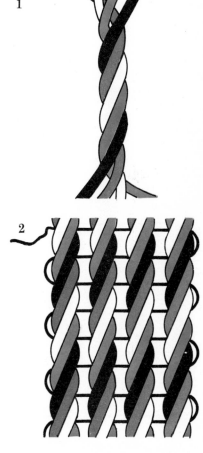

1

2

1. Four threads from each tablet twist together forming a spiral, rope-like structure.
2. The fabric is formed from a series of twisted threads joined by a weft.

71

3a. Draw in diagonals and rounded corners on tablets.
3b. Finished tablets have holes in corners and one in centre.
4. Pattern chart for watchstrap.

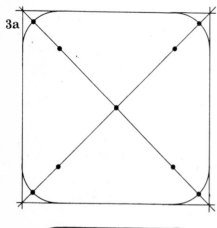

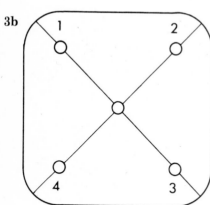

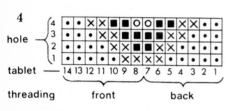

hole	14	13	12	11	10	9	8	7	6	5	4	3	2	1
4	•	•	×	×	■	■	○	○	■	■	×	×	•	•
3	•	•	•	×	×	■	■	■	■	×	×	•	•	•
2	•	•	•	•	×	×	■	■	×	×	•	•	•	•
1	•	•	•	•	•	×	×	×	×	•	•	•	•	•

tablet

threading   front   back

• black 28 threads   ■ green 10 threads

× red 16 threads   ○ white 2 threads

The entire set of tablets is turned through an angle of 90° (one quarter turn of a square tablet) between each pick of weaving. The continual turning of the tablets causes the lengthwise threads to wrap around each other and the rows of closely packed spirals give this type of weaving its characteristic appearance. All the colour is supplied by the warp threads, the weft is hidden except for a very little at the edges of the spirals.

The watchstrap

This decorative watchstrap, 18mm (¾in) wide, can show off the largest or smallest of watches.

Kits with ready-made tablets in plastic are available but it is a simple matter to make your own tablets to begin with.

To make the tablets and shuttle

Each tablet is a 5cm (2in) square, rounded at the edges with a hole close to each corner and another hole in the centre.

Rule off 14 5cm (2in) squares on the card as this is the number of tablets required in making the strap. Mark the centres of each square by drawing in diagonal lines and mark 3mm (⅛in) and 12mm (½in) in from the corners along these diagonal lines (fig.3a). Sketch around the edge of a coin on the 3mm (⅛in) mark and round off the corners to achieve the correct shape.

If you prefer, you can trace the shape of the tablet as shown in fig.3b. Cut out the tablets with care using the knife and ruler for the straight edges and scissors for the rounded corners. Using the 12mm (½in) mark, punch holes in each corner and also in the centre of each tablet (fig.3b).

Rub down all rough surfaces with a fine sand paper. The sides must be smooth for easy turning in the warp and there must not be any jagged edges to catch and snag the threads. Number the holes from 1 to 4 on one side of each tablet in a clockwise direction, starting in the top left hand corner.

It is a help to mark each outside edge of the tablets with a colour so that it is quickly seen if one of the tablets is out of place. Using a felt tipped pen is the easiest method, so apply a different colour on each of the four edges. Finally, make a shuttle to hold the weft yarn by tracing the shape (fig.3c). Use the same cardboard as for the tablets. Having cut the required number of tablets and the shuttle, lay them aside and prepare the yarns.

The warp

With 14 tablets, you will need 56 warp threads in all – four threads per tablet. When calculating the length of the warp, allowances

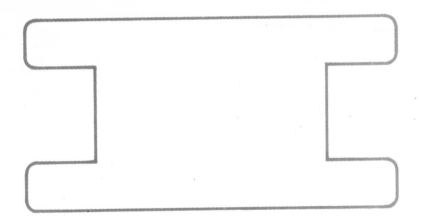

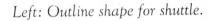

have to be made for wastage. Add two lengths of 15cm (6in) for the knots at each end, 30cm (12in) for the warp which cannot be woven and a further 18cm (3in) for 'take up' or loss in the actual weaving. In addition, you will need another 8cm (3in) for finishing off the strap. Therefore, for a 23cm (9in) strap you will need threads of 98cm (39in) length each.

The pattern chart

The pattern chart or draft (fig.4) tells a weaver everything he or she needs to know to make up a design. The number of tablets, the threading direction and the colour of the thread to go through each hole are all contained within the chart. Each square on the graph paper represents a hole and its respective colour thread.

Looking at the pattern chart, you will see that the watchstrap needs 28 black threads, 16 red, ten green and two white. Measure off and cut the required threads in each colour and place them in colour groups across a table or hang them over the back of a chair. Yarn tends to cling together and a pull on one thread often dislodges several more which can lead to knots, tangles and broken threads. Therefore, keep all the colours separate and later on keep all the groups of threads well away from the tablets already threaded.

Threading the tablets

Number the tablets in pencil from one to 14 and pile them in order, face upwards with number 14 on top of the pile. To thread them you will have to keep the pattern chart constantly to hand as a reference. Reading across, you will see that card 14 needs four black threads. Thread one black thread through each hole working from the front to the back (fig.5a). Pull about 23cm (9in) through each hole to the back of the tablet.

When each hole has been threaded, place the tablet on a table and

---

Watchstrap

You will need :
Fourteen tablets.
Card shuttle.
One ball each of black, red, green and white No.5 mercerized cotton.
Chair.
Ruler for beating down the weft.
Strong support such as a hook in the wall, a radiator pipe or a door knob. Three lengths of cord or strong string not less than 20cm (12in) long.
Needle for darning in ends.

Tablets and shuttle

You will need :
Sheet of smooth, thick cardboard. Mounting board is ideal and is generally available in art shops.
Scissors and sharp knife or scalpel.
Pencil and rubber.
Punch or gimlet to make a hole roughly the size of a No.8 (US6) knitting needle.
Fine sandpaper.
Felt tipped pens in four contrasting colours
Tracing paper.

5a. Threading from front
5b. Threading from back
6. Tablets secured with thread through centre hole.
7. Bind ends with cords.

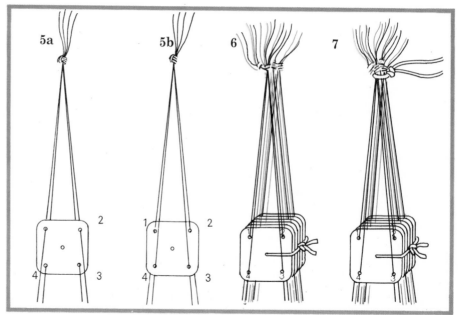

even up the four threads. Knot the four ends together at the back of the tablet about 5cm (2in) from the cut ends.

Thread tablet 13 following the colour chart in the same manner (four blacks). Place the tablet on top of tablet 14 so that the numbered holes match – one on one, two on two etc. Continue threading the tablets following the chart until tablet eight has been completed and laid on top of the pile on the table.

Threading back to front

Series of tablets are threaded in alternate directions, from front to back or from back to front (figs.5a and 5b). This ensures a clear, even braid and prevents the completed braid from curling up around its length, or distorting the weave.

In the watchstrap, half of the tablets are threaded from the front and half from the back. This is shown in the pattern chart. Thread tablets seven to one from the back (fig.5b) knotting the threads at the front. When all the tablets have been threaded and stacked, number one should be on the top of the pile facing upwards. Check that all the holes are in the correct position with hole one in tablet one on top of hole one in tablet two and so on down the pile.

Preparing the threaded tablets

Tie entire set of tablets together by passing a cord through the centre hole in the pile and tying the ends of the cord securely on the outside edge of the parcel of tablets (fig.6). Even up all the knotted ends and tie them together. This is done by binding another cord around all the warp threads just below the bunch of knots and tying it firmly so that none of the knots can slip (fig.7). Tie the ends of this securing cord to a strong support such as a door.

Stretch the warp gently until it is taut and evenly tensioned. Ease the tablets along the warp until they are about 30cm (12in) from the unknotted ends. If there are any twists or tangles, use your fingers as a comb and gently pull them through the threads. When the threads are straight and tensioned, knot all the ends together, bind another cord around the warp above the knot and tie it to the weaver's chair. The shuttle carries the weft thread through the warp to form a woven fabric. Wind the shuttle evenly with black thread and place it ready for use.

Weaving

As with all forms of weaving, it is very important that the warp threads are kept taut and evenly tensioned. With one end of the warp attached to a strong support and the other attached to a chair, the tension on the warp threads can be adjusted by moving the chair. You will soon learn how to do this.

Take up a comfortable position with the warp directly in front as in the photograph. The marked face of the tablets should be facing to the right. Check this to make sure.

When the tension is correct, untie the centre string that is securing the parcel of tablets. It is immediately apparent that the warp is divided into two layers with two threads from each tablet in the upper layer and two in the lower. This forms the shed (figs.8a and 8b). You are now ready to start weaving.

Weaving now proceeds by turning the entire set of tablets forwards or backwards through a series of quarter turns. The shuttle carrying the weft yarn travels through the shed after each quarter turn. Practise the method on the watchstrap.

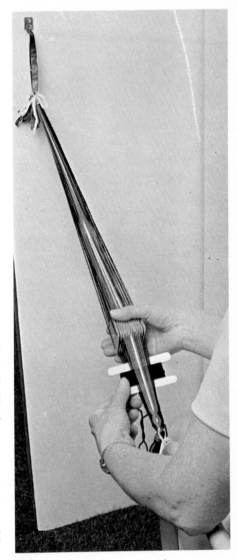

Threads kept in tension by stretching between a strong support (the door handle) and a chair.

Weaving the watchstrap

Before starting to weave, check the tension and make sure that the warp is divided into two layers. Hole one should be uppermost but furthest away. Insert the weft in the shed nearest you, allowing about 10cm (4in) to hang down. This end will be darned in when the weaving is completely finished.

Turn all the tablets one quarter turn (90°) towards you. Hole one will now be uppermost and nearest the weaver (fig.8a). Pass the weft through the new shed and press it down firmly. Use the edge of a ruler as a beater. After each turn, you should check that the shed is clear and that each tablet has turned. If the shed is not clear, gently slide the tablets up and down the warp or ease the tablets apart and let them fall back into place. Once turned, the tablets will remain in place. Turn the tablets another quarter turn towards you and pass the weft through the new shed. Beat it down.

Repeat this turning action twice more, passing the weft through the shed after each turn. Hole one will now be uppermost but furthest away from the weaver, ie in the original position. The first half of the pattern unit is complete after these four turns.

Completing the pattern

To weave the second half of the pattern unit, make four turns backwards away from you, inserting the weft after each turn (fig.8b). The pattern unit is thus completed in eight turns, four forward and four backward. You'll soon get used to the technique.

After a little practice it becomes easier to maintain a steady rhythm of turning, inserting the weft and beating down. Weave with four forward turns and four backward turns until the weaving measures approximately 7.5cm (3in) longer than the required length of strap. This additional length will be needed for finishing off.

To finish the watchstrap

Cut the weft yarn about 10cm (4in) away from the weaving. Darn in the end and finally trim. Darn the starting end of the weft into the fabric. Cut the warp at each end, about 12mm ($\frac{1}{2}$in) away from the weaving. Thread the braid through the strap bars of the watch and at one end attach the buckle by folding the cut ends of the weaving and making a hem in the usual way over the bar of the buckle. Finish off the other end with either a straight hem or by forming a point. To make a point, fold the fabric in half widthwise so that the right side is inside the fold and backstitch on the outside along the last weft thread.

Trim ends, turn right side out and press out the pointed end. Keep the tablets as they can be used successfully again and again.

8a

8b

8a. After one turn of the tablets forwards, Hole 1 is uppermost and nearest the weaver. 8b. Starting position for turning backwards away from the weaver. Hole 1 is uppermost but furthest away.

Designing with tablets

Weaving with tablets is as absorbing as any other form of weaving possibly because of, rather than in spite of, the limitations of width. Of course, it has the added attraction of being a type of weaving that needs no equipment other than cards and yarn.
The possibilities for pattern making are endless.
The width limitation of tablet weaving can also be its design strength for the harlequin effect of several related, but differently patterned, braids sewn together has an attractive peasant feel. You can sew as many braids as you like together to make bags, cushions, mats or even small scatter rugs. Individual braids can be used as belts, straps, hatbands, ties, chokers, watchstraps and table runners.
Perhaps the most attractive use of all for your braids is as trimmings for clothes and household objects. Sew braids onto cuffs, necklines, hems, pockets, bedspreads, curtains, or anything that needs a facelift. However, a word of caution – do be careful to select the right weight of braid for your fabric. A heavy wool braid would just not work on a lightweight fabric.

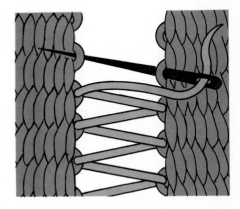

For a firm, invisible join between braids use a thread the same thickness as the weft. Thread your needle through the loops of weft at selvedges.

General hints

If you had difficulty in weaving the watchstrap you could have been making one of several mistakes common to beginners. Try to find out where you went wrong before you move on to the next stage of weaving braids to your own designs. Here are some general hints on tablet weaving that should help you to avoid mistakes and to create perfect braids.
Threading mistakes If the cards were threaded in the opposite directions from those indicated in the chart then a different twist effect would be produced and the pattern would be submerged. If the tablets were all threaded in the same direction, the pattern would be lop-sided with half of the design dominant. Threading all the tablets in the same direction also tends to encourage the completed braid to curl up around its length if the tablets are then turned all the same way. This varies with the type of yarn used as some curl around more than others.
Keeping an even width It is not always easy to keep the weaving

Above: Spectacle case made from wide braids.
Right: Sew braids together to make a casual bag.

an even width but any difficulty can soon be put right if care is taken to press the weft firmly and evenly into place. Draw the weft through the shed just enough to bring the warp threads together to cover the weft yarn and to give a firm, straight edge.

Do not hold the tablets too tightly together or they will be difficult to turn. They should be controlled but not pressed so tightly together that they do not hang free of each other. Always secure the tablets with the cord through the centre hole when weaving is interrupted to prevent misplacement.

Length of the warp There is always a certain amount of wastage for which allowance must be made when working out the length of the warp threads. In calculating the length of warp necessary for a finished braid of a definite length, remember to add two lots of 15cm (6in) for the knots at each end and 30cm (12in) for the end of the warp which cannot be woven.

A further generous allowance must be added for the take-up during weaving. This varies with the material used and the closeness of the weaving but 15cm (6in) is a good average.

Correcting mistakes If a mistake in the pattern has been made it can be rectified by turning the tablets in reverse. The warp will untwist and the weft can be drawn out.

Tablet weaving is not easy to undo, so you should watch the pattern carefully and you should not rely entirely on counting.

Finishing off To finish off your braids many different methods are open to you: simple sewing with an interesting stitch such as buttonhole, overhand knots, wrapping and tassels, plaiting or twining. Sometimes, the nature of the design will suggest the finish – a three-way pattern ending in three plaits for instance.

Pattern making

By using different coloured yarns and weaving to a definite order, a great variety of patterns can be obtained. There are various steps in designing your own patterns each of which are important if your final braid is going to turn out exactly as you imagine it.

Width The number of tablets and thickness of the yarn determine the width of the fabric. Twenty-four tablets threaded with no.5 cotton for instance, or 16 tablets threaded with four-ply knitting wool will, if correctly woven, make a 2.5cm (1in) band.

Choosing yarns Practically any yarn may be used, but it must be strong enough to withstand the constant twisting. It also needs to be smooth and easy running. Fuzzy and knobbly yarns do not give good results and can be difficult to work with as the fibres will cling together. Medium-weight mercerized cotton is recommended for beginners but wool, cotton, silk, nylon and other man-made yarns can all be put to good use in this type of work.

Colour All the colour is supplied by the length-wise warp threads. The weft is not visible except for a very little at the edges. Colour plays an important part in planning a pattern. Many arrangements are possible, of course, but the colour of the actual pattern should be in sharp contrast to the background. Brilliantly coloured pattern units on a dark or light background are the most effective.

Number of tablets

When you have chosen your yarn, you will have to find out how many tablets you will need to create a band of a particular width. Each card adds to the width of the fabric and a rough assessment of the width per card can be made by twisting two strands of your chosen yarn together. Measure the width of the twisted strands. This will be added by each tablet to the total width of the band.

Therefore, if your two fibres measure 1.5mm ($\frac{1}{16}$in) you will need 16 tablets to make a band 2.5cm (1in) wide. This is only a rough guide and the tension of the twisted threads must be the same as the tension achieved when weaving if it is to be at all accurate. Experience is the only real guide.

Working out a design

All patterns are worked out on squared paper. Each square represents one thread. Each vertical column of squares represents the four holes in each tablet and are numbered from one to four correspondingly. The number of tablets required is indicated along the bottom of the chart and the symbols show the colour of each thread. The threading direction of the tablets is also shown, and the colour key with the required number of threads is shown with each chart. Look at the diagrams carefully before you start.

Drawing up drafts Take a piece of graph paper (or square off a plain piece). Follow the patterns here as a guide.

It is easier to start designing for yourself with only two colours but even with two you can achieve many interesting variations. The design of a braid is dictated by various factors: the colours and their arrangement, the threading direction of the tablets, and the turning sequence when weaving. It is because of these variables that so many different patterns can be produced with this simple technique.

Basic braids

The pattern charts for the basic braids shown here are given in figs.1 to 5. They show vertical and horizontal lines (figs.1 and 2), spots (fig.3), chevrons (fig.4) and triangles (fig.5). The tablets are threaded in the direction shown in the respective charts and weaving proceeds by turning the tablets forwards and towards the weaver. Each pattern repeat is completed in four turns and all the basic braids are woven with the tablets being turned all one way. If the tablets were turned four turns each way as in the watch-strap, a mirror image would be formed. Only the straight line of basic braid (fig.1) would remain the same if the tablets were reversed.

Unfortunately, turning the tablets all one way causes the threads at the back of the tablets to become twisted and weaving will eventually have to stop while they are straightened out. There are two ways of correcting this trouble.

Preventing tangles: untying warp The first is to tie the set of tablets together using the centre hole and to untie the warp ends from the strong support. Straighten the threads, retie and continue weaving. In this way, weaving will produce a repeat of the first pattern unit so that the simple pattern repeat of the braids in

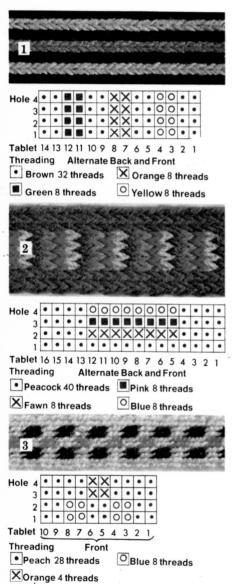

Hole 4 3 2 1
Tablet 14 13 12 11 10 9 8 7 6 5 4 3 2 1
Threading   Alternate Back and Front
• Brown 32 threads   ✕ Orange 8 threads
■ Green 8 threads   ○ Yellow 8 threads

Hole 4 3 2 1
Tablet 16 15 14 13 12 11 10 9 8 7 6 5 4 3 2 1
Threading   Alternate Back and Front
• Peacock 40 threads   ■ Pink 8 threads
✕ Fawn 8 threads   ○ Blue 8 threads

Hole 4 3 2 1
Tablet 10 9 8 7 6 5 4 3 2 1
Threading   Front
• Peach 28 threads   ○ Blue 8 threads
✕ Orange 4 threads

figs.1 to 5 are produced. This is the more complicated method.

Changing direction of turning The second method is by changing the direction of the turning. This method is easier and much more commonly used. This is to turn the tablets in the opposite direction away from the weaver, after the turns forward. A set pattern of turning forward and away is used as when weaving the watchstrap. If the tablets are turned in the opposite direction, the twisted threads behind the tablets naturally unroll and weaving can go on without interruption. At the same time the pattern changes on both the right and the wrong side of the braid. The basic pattern is reversed to give a mirror image when the tablets are turned in the opposite direction. The change in the direction of turning the tablets and the resulting change in the pattern formation is a particular feature of tablet weaving.

Variations in turning

One of the most exciting aspects of tablet weaving is the number of different patterns that can be achieved simply by altering the method of turning. The tablets can be turned in any number of repeating sequences, four forwards and four backwards, six each way, ten, 20 and so on.

Shed sequence The forward and backward method offers unlimited opportunities for pattern variations, depending on which shed is used for the change in the direction of turning. Even if you choose the normal four turns each way you can achieve different patterns depending on the shed that is first used.

Threading direction

Perhaps the most difficult aspect of designing for tablet weaving is the threading direction of the tablets. Tablets are threaded from the front to the back or from the back to the front of the tablet. It must be remembered that all four yarns in a single tablet must be entered from the same direction otherwise it will be impossible to turn the tablets during weaving.

In the watchstrap the threading direction of the 14 tablets formed a system of seven forward and seven backward. This was determined by the directional pull of the pattern. The purpose of threading a set of tablets from opposite directions is to ensure an even braid with clear pattern units. For instance, using the chevron pattern (fig.4) as a guide, you will see the two lines of the chevron coming together in the point. The threads in tablets one to six should be threaded from back to front to give an inward slant and tablets seven to 12 should be threaded from front to back to get a similar inward slant to the point of the chevron shape.

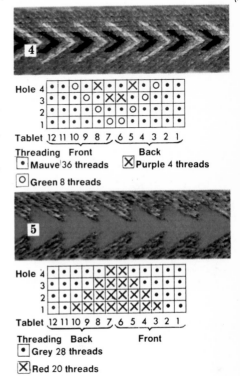

Inkle weaving on a loom

Although the origin of the word is unknown, an inkle is a coloured linen tape or braid rather like the braids produced in tablet weaving. Like tablet weaving, inkle weaving is restricted to narrow widths but weaving on a loom is much quicker and easier.

If you enjoy creating braids it may be worth buying an inkle loom. Although the pattern variations are not quite so numerous as in tablet weaving, inkle weaving on an inkle loom is an immensely satisfying type of weaving. Samples and braids in this chapter were all made on an inkle loom and they show some of the basic patterns that can be achieved by this method.

Inkle fabric

Inkle bands are extremely strong and hardwearing. They can be used for such things as belts, ties, bag-handles, head bands and guitar straps. If the strips are joined together with a flat stitch they make attractive articles including floor rugs, bags, cushions, ponchos, chair seats and stool covers. Inkle strips, of course, make excellent trimmings and are very useful for joining narrow strips of weaving together to make an attractive striped fabric.

Warp faced Like braids woven by tablet weaving, inkles are usually warp faced ie the warp is dominant, unlike tapestry where the weft is dominant. The warp threads are packed together so tightly that the weft does not show and to make an inkle the warp has to be held under a tension that is variable and controllable. This is because there is a great warp 'take up' and the tension has to be adjusted during weaving. To speed up the weaving process, there must also be some way of separating the two sheds.

The inkle loom

Because of all these requirements, a loom has evolved specifically for inkle weaving. Although inkles can be woven on more complicated looms, the inkle loom itself is very cheap and can be home-made. However, the construction must be very sturdy because there is great tension in the stretched warp.

There are at least two ready-made models on the market (figs.1 and

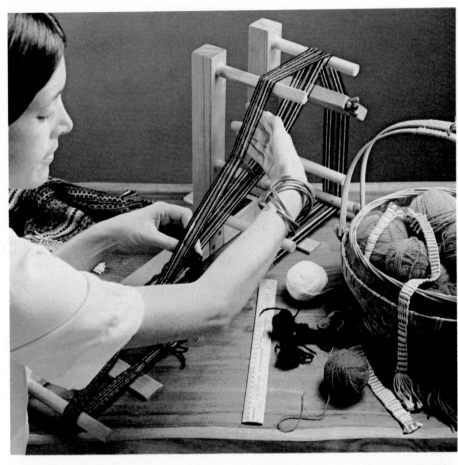

Weaving braid on the table model. Shed 1 is being made by pushing down on all the 'open' threads.

Making shed 2 lifting up all the 'open' threads.

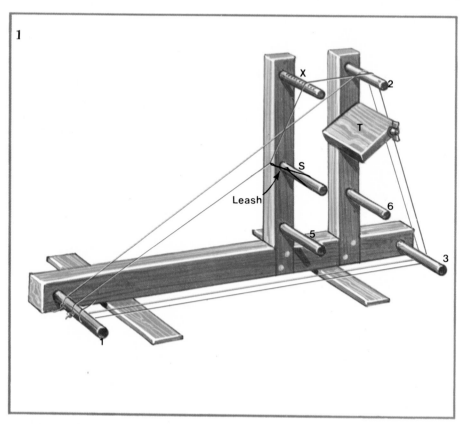

The table top inkle loom. Every other warp thread goes through a leash and over peg X. The other 'open' threads go straight round pegs 1,2 and 3.

2). The peg or flap T is important because it allows you to adjust the tension of the warp as the fabric is produced.

Materials

It is advisable for beginners to start with a strong, smooth thread such as mercerized cotton in bright colours. Once experience has been gained, a variety of yarns can be used including wool (woollen or worsted), silk, linen, rayon and nylon. In fact experiments can be made with new materials as you discover them or even as they are invented. Strong, textured threads and metallic threads can be introduced effectively. As in tablet weaving avoid using soft, hairy materials in the warp for they tend to cling together and make weaving difficult and tedious.

If mixing types of threads in the warp first test their elasticity and try to work with threads which will keep an even tension unless a 'seersucker' effect is required.

Winding the warp

The warp is wound straight onto the loom. One thread is taken straight round the pegs (one, two, three in fig.1 and one, two, three,

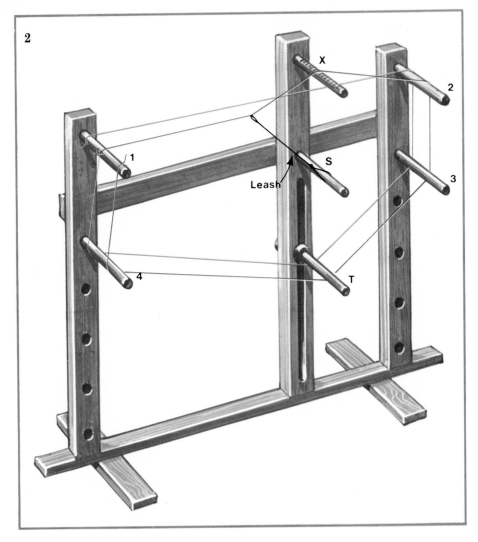

Longer braids can be woven on the floor model inkle loom by altering the position of pegs 3 and 4 to make a longer warp.

four in fig.2). The adjacent thread has to go through a string or cotton leash and over the notched peg (X in figs.1 and 2). If the loom does not have leashes attached to the peg they can be made as required by cutting equal lengths of about 20cm (8in) and tying them around peg S. Make a small loop at the end and they can become a permanent fixture on your loom. Make sure that your leashes are equal or your shed will not be clear. Warp threads that go straight around the pegs are called 'open' and can be raised or lowered by hand to create the two sheds needed for weaving.

Length of warp The length of the warp can be adjusted on the bigger model (fig.2) by altering the position of pegs three and four. This will give the warp threads a longer or a shorter journey. On the smaller model (fig.1) there are two extra pegs (five and six) which

85

are supplied to extend the length of the warp.

Remember to add at least 30cm (12in) to the length of the strip required when calculating the length of the warp because it is not possible to weave right to the end of the warp and you lose length in the take up. The beginning and end of the warp cannot be woven. It takes about 2.5cm (1in) at the beginning to settle the width of the braid and the end cannot be woven because the leashes always tend to get in the way.

Width of warp In inkle weaving the weft is pulled tightly and the warp threads are consequently drawn in. This will reduce the width of the braid to about half of that originally shown when the warp is wound on. Do not worry about the sett of the warp as in this particular form of weaving the weft pulls the warp into a close position automatically. The width of the weaving is determined by the thickness of the warp threads so that ten coarse threads will give a wider fabric than ten fine threads.

Putting on the warp Attach the end of the first thread to peg one making a knot which can be untied easily. Wind the threads according to the colour scheme changing colours at peg one by tying the new colour to the old one securely. Thread one thread right around the loom and the next one through a leash and so on until all the threads are on – with every other one through a leash. After all the threads have been warped, cut the last warp end about 15cm (6in) beyond peg one. Undo the knot securing thread one and

1. A simple braid of lines and stripes woven in two-ply worsted wool.
2. The same with the selvedge and weft in blue
3. Two blue threads substituted for two red ones to make alternate bars

tie the thread to the last thread. With very wide inkles it would be advisable to tie thread one to thread four or five and the last thread to one which is about four or five threads in from that end. This prevents the warp from being distorted. As the whole warp is going to travel around the pegs during weaving in a kind of un-rolling motion, it must not be anchored to any of the pegs.

Even tension The warp threads must be of an even tension. If the last part of the warp is tighter than the first part, the weaving itself will be crooked. Adjust the tension by working the slack around until you have made sure the warp is even.

Short-cuts There are various ways of putting on the warp and after a little practice you will devise your own short-cuts. For instance, if winding a warp with alternate colour threads, you do not need to cut the yarn each time but simply take the two threads and wind them around together putting one colour through the leash and the other right around the loom.

Weaving

The width of the material is controlled by the weft and the density of the fabric is determined by the way in which the weft is beaten. As inkle fabrics are warp faced the weft should pull the warp threads closely together. In order to do this, and to get a good firm selvedge it is advisable to weave one pick, change shed and then pull the weft thread tightly before weaving the second pick.

4. Braid using dashes, alternate dashes and lines in two-ply wool the last few rows of weft pulled in tightly

5. Same warp, different weft. Design is made up of alternate bars and lines

6. Braid of bars and lines with the last few rows of weft pulled in tightly

To weave on an inkle loom you may like to use a small stick shuttle. Alternatively, wind your yarn into a lozenge shape and use a thin stick such as a ruler for beating down.

Changing sheds To make the two sheds you simply lift or press down on the open threads as shown in the photographs. As they move you create the two sheds – one with the open threads above, one with the open sheds below.

When weaving, it is useful to get into the rhythm. You will develop your own method of working but one useful way is to push the open threads down with the right hand when weaving from left to right and lifting the open threads with the left hand when weaving from right to left. As you weave, pull the whole warp around the loom until you get back to the beginning again.

Reading a draft

The basic pattern charts are shown in figs.1 to 6 and the braids featured show how you can combine even the most basic pattern structures to create interesting effects.

The charts should be read from left to right because the loom is threaded in this direction. Only the threads which are needed to show the basic pattern unit are on the chart. To make a wider band, repeat the pattern unit across. The lower line shows the threads which go straight round the loom or the 'open' threads. The upper line shows the threads which must be taken through the leashes. The chart also shows you the ultimate form that the design will take as your braid will be a constant repeat of the pattern in the chart. When the odd numbered threads are pushed down, the even numbers will show on the surface of the cloth and vice versa. The whole of the design is created by the warp threads.

The braids

All the braids shown are easy to weave on an inkle loom. They show combinations of basic braid designs and give some ideas for colour schemes. If you would like to make up any of the braids, simply follow the relevant pattern draft and notes on weaving materials needed for the individual braid.

Tension of weft By altering the tension of the weft you can change the width of your braid. Pulling the weft tightly will narrow the braid and a slackened weft will produce a fan shape.

Finishing off On an inkle, there is a large number of warp ends, so it is necessary to think of ways of making the weft secure. The usual overhand knot would probably be too bulky in most cases. However, it is possible to braid the fringes, wrap them or twist them. The samples have a weft darned in leaving a fringe.

1. Stripes

2. Dashes

3. Alternate dashes

4. Line

5. Bars

6. Alternate bars

1-6. The basic design elements. Top line in each represents leash threads and bottom line the open threads.

Opposite: Floor rug made from 12 braids. Each braid was woven with two-ply rug wool.

Designing
inkle braids

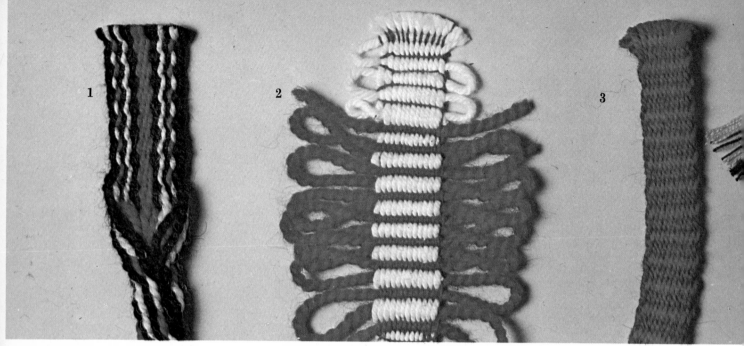

1. Part of the braid woven into a tube
2. A pattern of alternate bars of colour with a double weft used to create a picot edges.
3. Four closely related colours are used for this braid which is pulled into a curve at the lower end of the weaving.

After a little practice on the inkle loom designing your own inkles is very simple. As an inkle is a warp-faced fabric, the choice and arrangement of colours in the warp is extremely important for this is what provides the design. Gay, contrasting colours are always useful with black and white helping to outline the effects.

Texture can be obtained by using thick and thin, dull and shiny, fancy spun or plain threads. A braid can be completely transformed by using a thick weft, for instance, or by substituting two silver warp threads for two wool ones.

The weft should be a little coarser than the warp but as it is almost completely covered, its colour is unimportant. However, it will show very slightly at the edges of the braid and it is advisable to warp four threads at either side of the inkle in the same colour as the weft. If this rule is not followed, you will get a spotted effect on the side of your braid which will spoil the effect.

Planning Squared paper is invaluable for all warp plans. Remember to think of the warp in pairs – one open and one through the leash. If you make proper warp charts on squared paper (figs.1 to 6) you will have a useful record of your braid designs.

Ideas for braids Even though 10cm (4in) is about the widest braid that can be produced on an inkle loom, there is certainly no reason why braids cannot be sewn together to create wider fabrics. The

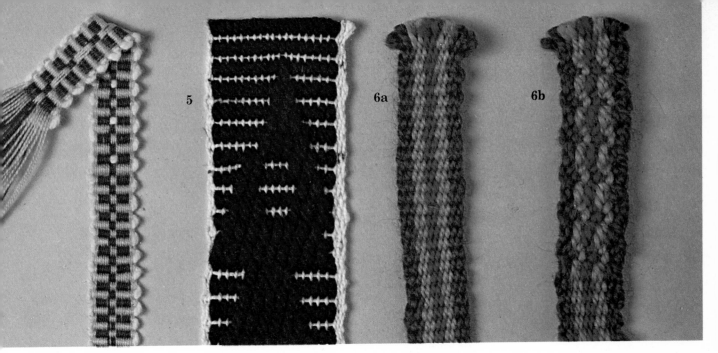

5   **6a**   **6b**

rug illustrated was made up from 12 wide braids of related patterns and colour schemes. For another experiment, you could make a bag of four braids, which you then cut in half widthwise, and sew up together lengthwise. It is really just a matter of using your imagination, the uses for braids are limitless.

Varying patterns
Never be afraid to experiment with your braids, for, as with all weaving, there are really no limitations.

Tubular weave To create a tubular effect (fig.1) weave the band using the normal two sheds but always place the weft in the shed from the same side and pull it tightly. Do not work too close to the leashes. The first weft pick is entered from either the left or right side and then taken back underneath the weaving to the side you started. Pull tightly and weave the next pick from the same direction. This process naturally pulls the braid into the tube. You can return to normal plain weave at any time.

Picot looped edges (fig.2) can be woven by using two wefts – a thick and a thin one – simultaneously. The thick thread forms the loop while the fine thread is woven plain to pull in the selvedge and to keep the braid firm and secure.

A curved end (fig.3) can be formed by pulling the end warp

4. Pick-up patterning used in the top half of the braid to introduce the white weft into the main body of the braid.

5. Pick-up technique used to create a motif. By picking up the black open threads and introducing them into the white leashes, shapes can be made. Before weaving, work out on paper which threads you will pick up in each row.

6a, 6b. Both braids woven using the same yarn and warp chart. 6b is woven using the twisted warp technique described overleaf.

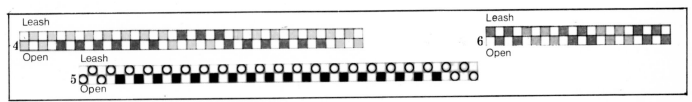

threads after the braid has been taken off the loom. Pull the warp ends in the inside curve harder than the ones towards the outside of the curve. Darn in the weft securely before pulling the ends.

The Ghiordes knot can be introduced into the warp for extra texture. Always strengthen the braid with a few picks of plain weave introduced between rows of knots.

Pick-up designs

The simplest method of adding extra interest to a design is to make some of the weft thread show in the actual pattern. This is done by forming a gap in the lower shed threads where the weft will be exposed and become a feature of the pattern.

To do this you have to pick up the relevant lower threads and incorporate them in the upper shed. This will have the effect of allowing the weft colour to show in the reverse of the braid and to introduce the lower shed colour out of sequence on the right side of braid. This can be done in a regular pattern (fig.4) or in a shape (fig.5). Either method produces attractive results.

On the top part of the yellow and black braid (fig.4) the pick-up technique is used to introduce the white weft into the main body of the braid. The three centre yellow threads that appear in the open line of the working chart are picked up and woven with the leash threads in a regular pattern. The reverse side of the braid shows the three threads floating on the surface. The black and white braid (fig.5) uses a warp of thick black cotton with fine white cotton. Woven normally and using the white cotton as weft results in a pattern of thick and thin alternate bars. By picking up the black open threads and introducing them into the white leash threads, shapes can be made. Because the black cotton is so thick it completely obscures the white leash threads giving a raised motif. Before weaving a shape, work out on paper which threads you will wish to pick up in each row.

Twisted warp

Another technique that can be used to vary your braids is to twist the warp. The texture and pattern of a braid can alter radically if a twist is introduced into the warp threads (fig.6)

When the open threads are up, twist the right-hand open thread under the left-hand leash thread and pick up the open thread on the other side (fig.7). Continue in this manner all the way across the warp for that pick. Weave the return pick normally. Weave the next pick and every alternate pick using the twisting technique. This is a particularly good technique for subtly altering the patterning on a long braid. Sections can be woven alternately.

7

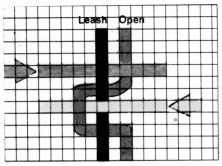

Leash   Open

Twisted warp technique: to add interest to a braid, twist the right hand open thread under the left hand leash thread and weave a pick.

Jacket on a frame loom

The versatile frame loom is not only useful for weaving tapestries. Imagination and a touch of improvisation can turn it into a piece of equipment as useful as the sewing machine. Chunky tapestry type clothes such as the ethnic-look jacket shown can be quickly and easily made up using the loom. Each pattern piece has totally straight edges so that no complicated shaping is necessary.

The jacket is made up by alternately weaving with ordinary yarn and unspun fleece. The fibres of the fleece are very soft and loose as they have not gone through the process of being twisted into yarn. When weaving the jacket the loose fibres are caught firmly

Jacket
You will need : 400g (14oz) of 2-ply wool yarn with a count of about 6. 250g (10oz) of wool top. Cold water dye. Frame loom with shed stick. Stick shuttle, tapestry bobbin or carpet needle for weaving. Darning needle. Silk or polyester sewing thread.

The jacket sleeves are shown already completed and ready on the larger size frame.

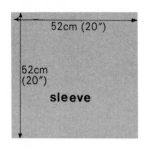

1a

52cm (20")

52cm (20")

sleeve

52cm (20")

52cm (20")

sleeve

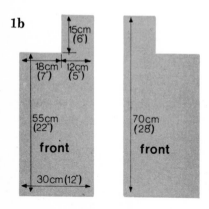

1b

15cm (6")

18cm (7") 12cm (5")

55cm (22")

front

30cm (12")

70cm (28")

front

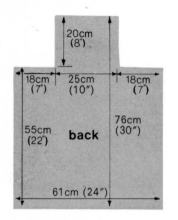

20cm (8")

18cm (7") 25cm (10") 18cm (7")

55cm (22") **back** 76cm (30")

61cm (24")

into the fabric by both the warp and the weft yarn. This creates the squared effect of the final fabric.

Wool top This is the term for prepared fleece that has been carded commercially and is ready to be spun into yarn. It comes in long strips with all the fibres running in the same direction. It is also sometimes called sliver or rovings by suppliers. Obviously, different tops are of different qualities and textures ranging from quality long fibre wool in worsted top to unusual unspun fibres such as yak and camel-hair. They are fun to try out.

Dyeing Most tops come in the raw colour of the fleece and you will have to dye it to the colour you wish before weaving. Use a commercial cold water dye to produce an all-over dye such as the colour on the jacket shown or random dye for a variegated appearance. Be very gentle with the fibres when dyeing and try to keep them in their parallel state. You may find that the natural colour of wool top is just right for a jacket. Make sure that you wash it before you weave if you do not wish to dye it.

The jacket

This warm and highly unusual jacket will fit most adults.

Frame loom To weave the pattern pieces as shown in fig.1 and the photographs, you will need a frame loom that is 80cm by 130cm (32in by 52in). If you have no frame you can easily make one up to these proportions by following the instructions given in the tapestry chapter. When you come to knocking the nails into the cross-pieces, put them in at 8mm (⅓in) intervals instead of the 12mm (½in) intervals stated.

If you already have the frame made in the tapestry chapter, an adaptation of the pattern will be needed as the frame is slightly too small to weave the back and sleeve widths (fig.1). In this case weave both the back and each sleeve in two pieces (fig.2). If you have not already knocked nails into the reverse side of the cross-pieces of your loom do so at 8mm (⅓in) intervals.

Jacket pattern All the pieces are made up of straight lines and as the jacket is loose fitting it has the added advantage of fitting most adults or else it can be easily adapted.

The back Take an end from two balls of your two-ply wool so that the two strands run parallel and you have the wool doubled. If you have the large frame, warp up 16cm (24in) with the doubled wool for a sett of three ends per 2.5cm (1in). Do this by winding the doubled wool once around every other nail. Do not forget to add an extra thread at each side for the selvedge.

If you have the small frame, warp up only 30cm (12in) in the same way. Use the centre 30cm (12in) of your frame.

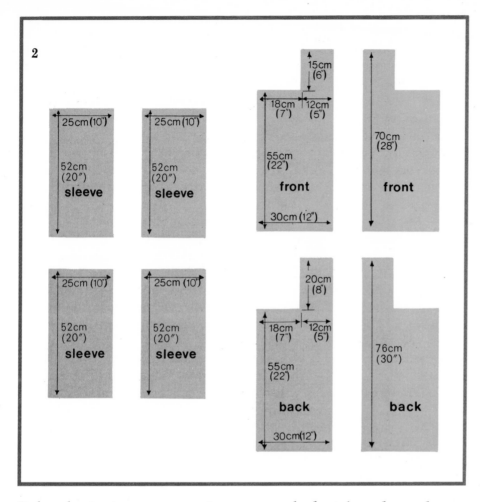

2

25cm (10")

52cm
(20")
sleeve

25cm (10")

52cm
(20")
sleeve

15cm
(6")

18cm   12cm
(7")   (5")

55cm
(22")

front

30cm (12")

70cm
(28")

front

25cm (10")

52cm
(20")
sleeve

25cm (10")

52cm
(20")
sleeve

20cm
(8")

18cm   12cm
(7")   (5")

55cm
(22")

back

30cm(12")

76cm
(30")

back

Opposite: The pattern pieces that can be woven on a large loom. All the pieces are made up from straight lines so the weaving is very simple.
1a. Pattern pieces for sleeves.
1b. Front pieces and back.

2. Alternative pattern for weaving on a small frame. The sleeves and back are woven in two parts and sewn together to make up the jacket.

Before beginning to weave, insert your shed stick under and over each double thread. Use leashes if you wish to speed up your weaving or if you prefer to use them.

Weaving the back Throughout all the weaving, the yarn is used double. Double the yarn and wind up a shuttle or bobbin. If you do not have either of these pieces of equipment, use a large needle such as a carpet needle or wind the yarn into a lozenge shape.

Weave about six rows with the yarn. Each pattern piece begins and ends with these few rows of yarn. This not only gives a firm edging but it also helps to bring all the warp threads into an even position. When weaving, every other pick can be quickly done by lifting the shed stick to give you a clear open shed. The return pick has to be done in the normal way unless you have added leashes to your frame to speed up your work.

After these first few rows, lift the shed stick ready to introduce the top and leave the yarn dangling at the side.

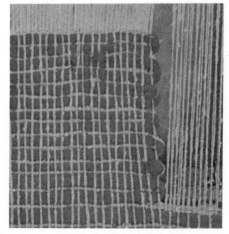

Above: Detail of shaping needed in front and back pieces.

Below: Separating the two sleeves woven on the larger frame by cutting the warp threads between them. Darn in all ends before sewing pieces together.

15cm (6")

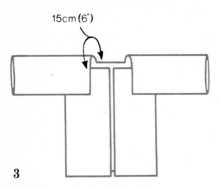

3

Above: How to sew the pieces together to make the jacket. 15 cm (6in) of each sleeve forms part of the square neckline over the shoulders

Take a strip of the top and divide into thin strips about the thickness of a finger. Do not make your strips longer than about 76cm (30in) or you will have difficulty in weaving. Introduce a thin strip of the top into the open shed created by the shed stick. Weave back the starting end for about 2.5cm (1in). Beat down with the bobbin or a ruler. Pick up the hanging yarn and weave one pick back. Lift the shed stick and weave back with the top.

Continue weaving with alternate rows of yarn and top, until you have completed 55cm (22in). The picks of yarn strengthen and neaten the fabric. Overlap the top neatly when you have to join two strips so that the joins are invisible.

After the 55cm (22in), continue weaving only the centre 25cm (10in) if you are using the larger frame (fig.1). If you are using the small frame, weave the right-hand 12cm (5in) (fig.2). Weave this area for a further 20cm (8in). Finish off with a few rows of yarn to form a firm edge. Cut weaving off the frame and darn in all loose ends including the warp ends. If you have the smaller frame, weave the second half of the back but this time weave the narrower part at the top on the left-hand side.

The front Weave the two front pieces in exactly the same way as the back but following the sizes indicated in the pattern (see fig.1 or 2). These two pieces will have to be woven separately whether you have a large or small loom. Make sure that you work from the same pattern throughout.

The sleeves The sleeves are perfectly square and if you have the large frame you can weave them on the same warp. After weaving the first sleeve of 52cm (20in) leave a short gap and begin weaving the second sleeve. With the smaller frame, you will need to weave all the sleeve pieces on separate warps.

Making up the jacket Darn in all loose ends and tidy up any top that is projecting by pushing it to the back of the fabric. Assemble all the pieces as in fig.3. When joining pieces together, you will not be able to turn under a seam as is usually done because the fabric is too thick. Simply use a strong silk or polyester sewing thread and oversew the pieces together with the right sides facing. Make sure that the needle goes under the double thread of the selvedge.

Sew the two back pieces together with a centre back seam and join the sleeve pieces to make a square if you are working from fig.2. Sew the side seams together. Fold the sleeves and sew the underarm for 32cm (13in). This will leave you 18cm (7in) for attaching the sleeves to the lower part of the shaped armholes in both back and front pieces. Sew the remainder of the sleeves to the armhole opening. This leaves 15cm (6in) which forms part of the square shape of the neckline (see fig.3).

Free form tapestry

Traditionally, tapestries were created using only the straight line technique described in making the tapestry sampler. However, only the purist believes that rules must never be broken and there are many interesting experiments which can be made simply by daring to try. Once you are relieved of the strictures of the straight line rule then a whole new area of tapestry design and picture making opens up for the weaving enthusiast.

The small tapestries shown here on pages 100 and 101, were made with the weft curving in a free fashion rather than working within a geometric grid. Without having to plan your cartoon in advance, the curving weft technique can allow you to create your tapestry on the frame, building up different areas until the whole design is formed in a spontaneous fashion.

1. Winding the warp around the small frame loom.
2. A piece of string brings all the threads together.

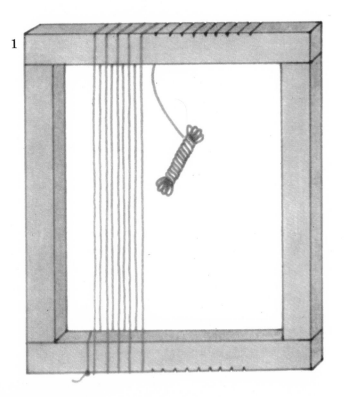

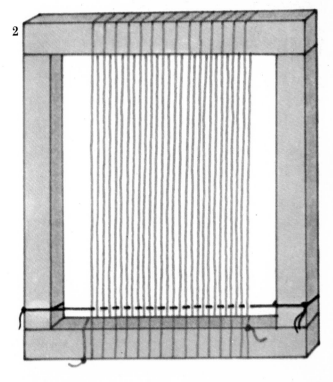

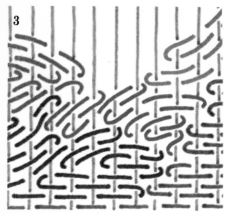

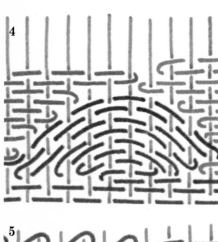

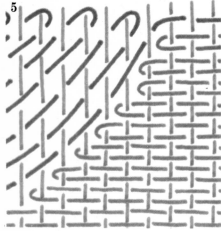

3. Free form weft areas
4. No interlocking necessary
5. Straight and curved weft

The following instructions give you the basic principles.

Materials

It is not only in the curving of the weft that these tapestries break the rules. They were made on a small picture frame 55cm by 48cm (22in by 19in) with the warp wrapped around the two cross-pieces. The size of the frame and the looseness of the weave compared with normal tapestry means that a lighter more attractive yarn can be used for the warp in place of the cotton or linen warp yarn usually used. A very fine string, button thread or even a mercerized cotton can act very satisfactorily as warp.

Putting on the warp Wind the cotton around the frame in a circular motion (fig.1). A good sett for such simple tapestries is four ends per 2.5cm (1in) so that there is ample room for experimenting with thick textural yarn. Wind the warp firmly but not too tightly as cotton does not have a great deal of elasticity. To keep the warp in place, it is a good idea to cut narrow grooves at intervals of 12mm ($\frac{1}{2}$in) so that each thread crosses over the frame in a groove (see fig.1). This secures the warp very firmly.

Colour of warp In free form tapestry, there is no necessity to cover the warp completely, in fact, sometimes you may find that the warp shows in spite of beating down. It is best to choose a thread for your warp in a colour which will blend in with your general colour scheme. This will allow you to use the warp as part of your design if you wish. When winding the warp, keep an even tension as you would when weaving a traditional tapestry.

As a small frame such as this will not take cross sticks without losing a lot of warp, use a piece of firm cotton twine or string to weave one row at the bottom of your frame and tie it to each side of the frame (fig.2). This will have the same effect as cross sticks in that all the threads will be evened out and brought together ready for weaving. You will save a lot of warp this way.

Weft Working on such a small scale, gives an ideal opportunity for using up any scraps of yarn you may have left over from other weaving or knitting projects. Small areas of weft are worked with tiny pieces of yarn and any type of yarn can be used from rug wool to knitting wool and all sorts of fancy yarn such as bouclé and mohair. All four tapestries shown were woven using knitting wools and crochet cottons of all different sorts and colours. Texture was built up with fancy yarn to create such areas as the knobbly field effect in the Summer tapestry. Strands of silver or gold thread can be very effective and, of course, handspun yarn, raw fleece or rag strips can be added for contrast. Because the warp is so fine, you may find it easier to use a tapestry needle.

Curving the weft

Basically, the curved weft is much easier to weave than the normal straight line designs as it can be allowed to grow in small areas as you work without any prior planning. The mixing of the yarns and the free form of the weft means that weaving is a matter of constantly compensating for a build-up in one area by weaving in extra yarn in the adjoining area. As you work on an area you can change colour when and where you like as in normal tapestry but, unlike normal tapestry, a piece of weft can be curved around a woven area. No weft interlocking is necessary as the threads are taken around adjoining warp threads and no long straight joins are formed (see figs. 3 and 4). Always maintain the under/over weaving sequences as much as possible. The firmness of your beating down can also vary the design with some areas packed down well and others much looser. Allow enough slack on each thread for the extra journey it will have to make around the other threads and beat down firmly. You will find that because of the fineness of the yarn in relation to the spacing of the warp and the curving of the weft, the warp may be difficult to cover and may show slightly between your weft. If this happens it is a wise idea to make the specks of warp a design feature and so use the fault creatively.

Always remember that you can only weave an area if the area underneath has already been woven.

Straight edge A problem which often occurs when weaving in this free way is that it is more difficult to keep a straight edge. If you find that your tapestry is curving badly at the sides it is probably because you are not allowing enough slack on your weft threads to compensate for the curving as well as the usual under/over take-up. Do make sure that you check your slack as you go.

Picture making

Curving the weft offers an ideal opportunity for creating pictorial tapestries as well as for more abstract designs. In the Four Seasons tapestries shown in this chapter, colour and shape combine to give an impression of a landscape at different times of year. This is further emphasized by the use of textured threads and the combinations of different types of wool to create a three-dimensional impression with a lot of texture and movement.

Because these tapestries are much more loosely woven than more conventional ones of rug wool, their use may be looked on as purely decorative. Perhaps the largest hanging that can be made with this sort of warp and weft combination would be about 60cm by 90cm (2ft by 3ft). However, there is absolutely no reason why you should not use a curved weft technique using conventional

---

Summer tapestry

You will need :
Small frame such as a picture frame not less than 55cm by 48cm (22in by 19in) and fairly strong in order to withstand the tension of the warp.
Ball of yellow mercerized crochet cotton or button thread.
20g ($\frac{3}{4}$oz) of mixed knitting or weaving yarns in a blue colour range.
35g ($1\frac{1}{4}$oz) of mixed knitting or weaving yarns in a yellow/orange colour range.
As you will need only short lengths of each colour, aim to use up scraps rather than buying a wide range of new wool. For instance, the black tractor image in the cornfield would only take about 90cm (36in) of yarn. Try also to get hold of textured yarns such as a bouclé for the fields or white slub for clouds.
Piece of cotton twine at least 52cm (20in) wider than your frame for the cross thread.
Tapestry needle for weaving and a tapestry bobbin or ruler for beating down.
Two thin dowel rods about 22cm ($8\frac{1}{2}$in) long and 1cm ($\frac{3}{8}$in) in diameter.
Piece of muslin interfacing for backing and fabric adhesive.

materials or in combination with traditional straight line techniques (fig.5). There will be no size restriction here except, of course, that imposed by the size of your frame loom.

The Summer tapestry

The Summer tapestry, second from left, is only 25cm by 18cm (10in by 7in) and was woven on a picture frame.

Warp up your frame as already described with a sett of four ends per 2.5cm (1in). Put in the cotton thread to bring all the warp ends together and to even out the spacing. Begin weaving with a few strengthening rows of straight tapestry.

After these first few rows, you are free to weave with whatever colours or yarn you have available to create the curving strata effect of the fields. The design is created both by the colour combinations and the flow of the curves. Follow the photograph of the

Summer tapestry as a guideline and refer to the preceding weaving hints, using your yarns as creatively as you like.

Two thirds of the way up your tapestry is a good asymmetrical point at which to introduce the sky. Do not forget that the sky can vary as much in colour as the land.

When you have finished your tapestry, cut the warp threads near to the frame and tie them in pairs firmly around the dowel rods so that the rods are almost touching the tapestry. Pull back all the warp ends so that the knots are pushed to the back of the hanging and the dowel rods fit closely to the tapestry. To finish off the back of the hanging cut a piece of interfacing to the size of the tapestry and cover one side with adhesive. Stick the interfacing to the back of the hanging catching all the warp ends under it. This will not only tidy up the reverse side of the tapestry but will also give it some extra weight so that it hangs well when on a wall.

Left to right: Spring, Summer, Autumn and Winter are depicted in these pictorial tapestries woven using the curving weft technique. Each one measures 18cm by 25cm (7in by 10in). They are based on a Four Seasons theme, although the instructions and materials given are for the Summer tapestry.

Weaving on a roller loom

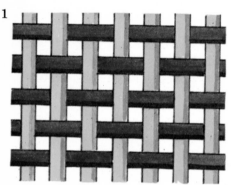

1

The basic plain weave structure

So far, all the chapters have dealt with building a fabric of limited length. Tapestry, tablet weaving and inkle loom weaving all have a warp the length of which is restricted by the size of the loom. However, the more general concept of handweaving is creating a longer fabric with a repeat design which can then be made up into anything you wish. For this you need a loom that will store a warp so that the fabric can be rolled up and more warp unrolled.

Plain weave (over one, under one) is built up by both warp and weft in equal proportion so that the pattern is a combination of colour from either direction (fig.1). Weaving lengths of cloth also differs from tapestry in that each weft pick is usually taken from edge to edge. Because of this repetitive action, a mechanical aid for making the sheds is incorporated in all looms to speed up production. Any such mechanical aid, whether a string leash on a frame loom or a wire one on a table loom, is known as a heddle. All such heddle systems are merely a sophisticated version of the simple leashes discussed earlier. Whatever loom you use from a small roller loom to a large pedal loom, the basic weaving principles and general techniques are the same.

The roller loom

The simplest of table looms, the roller loom illustrated here, provides the two sheds necessary to produce plain weave. For this it uses a hole and slot rigid heddle – a strip of metal with alternate holes and slots to separate the sheds (fig.2).

There is a roller at each end of the loom which stores the warp, and a frame over which the warp is unwound. The frame helps to keep the warp threads in constant tension.

The rigid heddle is pushed up or down to separate the two sets of threads (figs. 3 and 4) and some roller looms have a useful system of supports to help the shedding action and to leave the weaver with two free hands (see the photographs opposite). Many patterns can be achieved by using plain weave but the following chapter will discuss more complex weaves that need more than the two sheds. (Incidentally it is not impossible to make yourself a simple

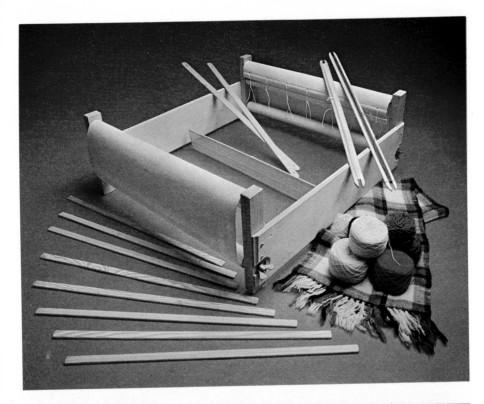

The roller loom is simply a
horizontal wooden frame with a
roller at each end for storing
the warp.

A more sophisticated roller loom
with a central support to help the
weaver push the heddle up
and down.

loom out of a good strong wood. This could be a useful way of saving money if you hope to advance to large looms.) Alternatively, you can buy a ready-made roller loom if you do not want to be too ambitious at present.

First steps

Once you have obtained your loom, the first step is to make a warp to put on it. Warp threads travel from the warp roller (or warp beam) through the heddle and onto the cloth roller (or cloth beam). Whatever loom you eventually choose, the method of making a warp will be the same although the larger the loom you use the easier it is to warp up the threads.

As the warp plays as much a part in the design of an object as the weft, it must be worked out before you start.

Plaid scarf

The plaid scarf is woven in plain weave and demonstrates the possibilities of pattern making with only two sheds. It is 29cm by 125cm (11½in by 50in), and is a good first project.

The warp

The length of the warp must be calculated before the warp can be made. As you have to allow a certain amount of warp to go over and under the weft threads, every 90cm (36in) is calculated at 100cm (40in). This is known as a weaver's metre or yard. When taken off the loom your weaving will spring back a bit and this shrinkage may be further aggravated when the fabric is washed. This means that for every 90cm (36in) an extra 10m (4in) must be woven. The warp for the scarf will also require the necessary extra length for tying onto the two rollers and for the warp that cannot be woven beyond the heddle. The extra needed is usually 45cm (18in). Therefore, for a finished scarf of 125cm (50in) you need a warp of 125cm (50in) plus 15cm (6in) to make the weaver's metre

Right: The rigid heddle has holes and slots for threads to go through.

2

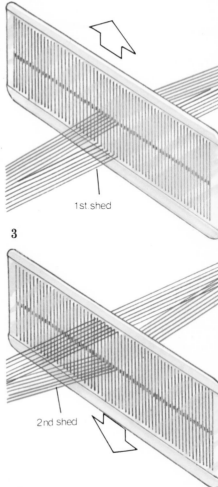

1st shed

3

2nd shed

4

3. When the heddle is pushed up the slots threads slide down to make shed 1.
4. When the heddle is pushed down the slot threads slide up to make shed 2.

Above and left: Beautiful soft furnishings such as the bedspread and cushion covers can be made in a plain weave pattern.

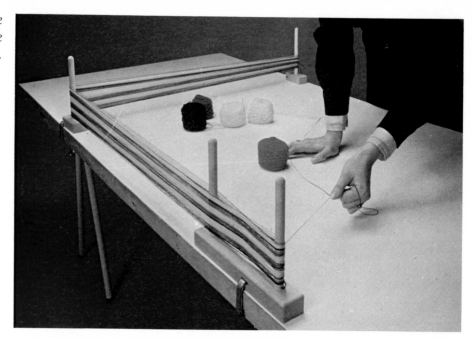

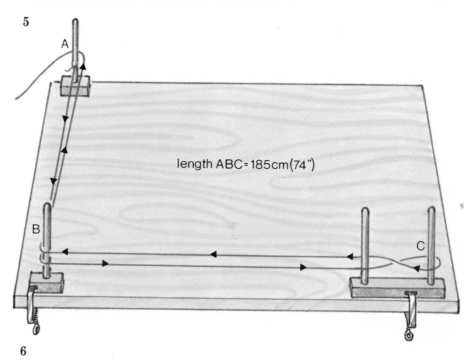

5

length ABC=185cm(74")

A

B

C

5. *How to wind the warp for the scarf. The distance between pegs A and C should be 185cm (74in)*
6. *The chart for the warp. When joining colours, knot at an end peg.*

6

7	6	6	26	6	6	6	26	6	6	6	26	6	6	7

or yard, plus 45cm (18in), making a total length of 185cm (74in).

Width of warp The width of the scarf has now to be calculated. As three-ply wool is being used the warp will be set at 13 ends per 2.5cm (1in). This is the usual spacing (dent) of the rigid heddle. Therefore, 29cm (11½in) at 13 ends per 2.5cm (1in) gives you 150 threads. You will also need an extra thread for the selvedge on each side. The total number of warp threads is 152.

Warping posts A warp is made by winding yarn to the correct length around warping posts. With a short warp such as this you can use three warping posts (two singles and one double). Warping posts (fig.5) are made from dowel rods inserted into blocks of wood and they can either be bought or made. They should be fixed to a solid table with G-clamps [C-clamps], so that the total distance between them is the length of one warp thread, ie 185cm (74in).

The yarn is wound around the posts so that two 185cm (74in) warp threads are completed with each full cycle. In this way all 152 threads are made in a continuous process of winding and then transferred together onto the loom.

The cross In fig.5 you will see that a cross has been made round the double end pegs. This is very important and each pair of warp threads must have its cross, otherwise you will find it considerably more difficult to put the warp onto the loom.

Warp colour To create the plaid pattern of the scarf, the warp threads vary in colour. Therefore, the threads must be wound between the warping posts in the correct order and the chart for the warp (fig.6) must be followed if the pattern is going to be successful in forming an even plaid.

Winding the warp With the warping posts positioned as in fig.5 take the black wool and wind around as shown. Each thread from one end peg to the other is one length, back is two and so on. Looking at the warp chart (fig.6) you will see that seven black threads are needed to begin winding the warp.

When you have wound seven black lengths, join the black to the red wool. The knot must be at an end peg and any break in your wool must be corrected by knotting at an end peg. Never have a knot in the middle as this will appear in your weaving.

After six red lengths, warp up six blue, then 26 yellow and continue to follow the chart until all 152 threads have been wound. Keep as even a tension as possible while winding between the posts. When you have 152 threads, tie off with a loop over whichever is the last post. Take a piece of string and drop it down through the back loop of the warp cross and then loop it under and up through the other side of the cross. Tie in a firm knot but leave a loop of string (fig. 7); so the warp cross is kept in the correct order.

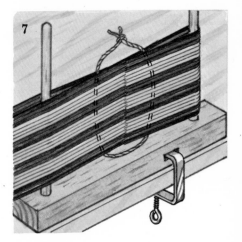

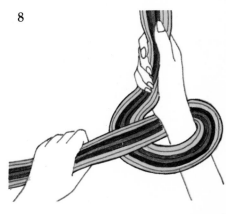

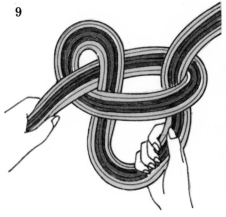

7. *Secure the cross with string.*
8. *Starting to chain*
9. *Pull warp through the loop*

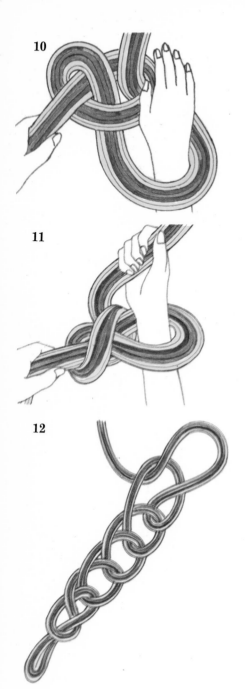

10

11

12

10. Put your hand through loop
11. Pull warp through loop
12. The chained warp.

Chaining up To keep the warp under control, it should now be chained up as shown in figs. 8, 9, 10, 11 and 12.

Carefully lift the warp off the peg away from the cross (peg A in fig.5). Leave it on the other pegs. Start chaining by positioning the warp across your wrist as shown in fig.8. Pull the warp through the loop over your wrist (fig. 9) and slip your hand through the new loop. (fig.10). Grasp the warp again to pull through the new loop (fig. 11), making the beginning of the chain.

This creates a chain (fig.12) and will stop your warp from getting tangled. When you reach peg B, lift the warp off the peg and continue chaining. Do not chain in the cross end.

Warping the loom

Getting the warp onto the loom may look a formidable task, but it can be a very absorbing one. The warp is 13 ends per 2.5cm (1in) and is now in a secure rope-like chain.

Take hold of the cross end of the warp and insert one of the sticks in the back loop of the tied cross. Clamp the stick to the table with two G-clamps [C-clamps].

Take two more of the sticks and bore a small hole in each end if they do not already have small holes. Insert one of the sticks in each loop of the cross (fig.13) and tie them together firmly so that there is about 5cm (2in) between the sticks. Remove the string tie holding the cross as it is now secured by the two sticks in each loop of the cross, these are called cross sticks.

Shake out the warp to roughly 29cm (11½in) in width and you will see that the warp threads run alternately under and over the cross sticks. The warp has now to be put into a raddle to space it over the correct width for the scarf.

Making a raddle

The raddle spreads the warp threads across the correct width and keeps them in the correct order throughout the weaving.

Take the piece of wood 2.5cm by 5cm (1in by 2in) by width of warp beam. Knock the 5cm (2in) wire nails into the wood at 12mm (½in) intervals but leaving the nails standing 3cm (1¼in) proud of the wood so that the raddle looks like a wide-toothed comb (fig.14).

Using the raddle As the raddle spaces are 12mm (½in) and the warp is 13 ends per 2.5cm (1in) the raddle spaces must hold six and seven threads alternately. Take the first seven black threads plus the next thread in correct order from the cross sticks. Place them in the first space of the raddle.

The extra thread (at each end) is for the selvedge so that the first and last space in the raddle has eight threads.

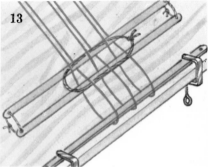

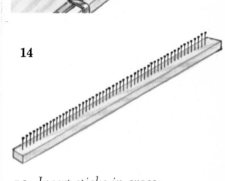

13. Insert sticks in cross
14. Knock nails into wood for
the raddle

Left: Weaving on the roller loom

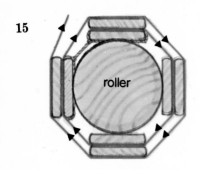

15

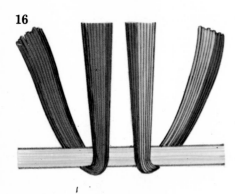

16

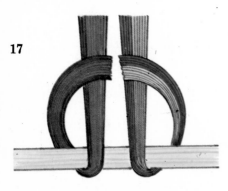

17

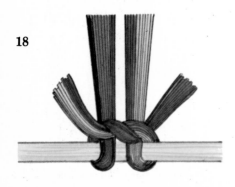

18

The next six threads go in the next space, the following seven threads in the next space and so on until all the threads are in the raddle. Make sure that all the threads are in the right order. Place rubber bands or a continuous thread over the nails to stop the warp coming out of the raddle. The bands should form a sort of lid. (Proper wooden raddles come with a removable wooden top).

The warp beam

Carefully remove the clamps holding the back stick to the table and take the whole of the warp to the loom. Tie the back stick firmly to the warp beam by means of strings or canvas apron ties.

Holding the warp firmly and at an even tension, wind it smoothly onto the warp beam. The raddle will comb it out to the correct width and the warp will unchain itself behind the hand you are using to hold an even tension. At this point, tension is all important and it is easier to wind the warp on if somebody helps you. One person should roll the warp onto the beam while the other holds the threads in tension combing with the fingers if any tangles should appear in the warp threads.

To keep the warp smooth, thin sticks called warp sticks should be wound around with the warp onto the beam. Always put each circuit of sticks on top of the previous sticks (fig.15). This prevents the sticks themselves distorting the warp.

When the warp is on the beam except for the last 45cm (18in), stop. Remove the remaining warp from the raddle and cut the end loops of about 20 of the threads. Tie these threads together in a loose overhand knot so that you do not lose the cross sticks and, thereby, the cross which will help you in threading the heddle.

Repeat this with groups of about 20 threads all across the warp.

Threading the heddle

Tie the rigid heddle in place on the loom so that the warp ends can be threaded through the holes and slots.

If you are using a 30cm (12in) heddle three spaces must be left empty on each side. If your heddle is much wider than 29cm (11½in), mark the centre space and count outwards 75 spaces to each side (count both holes and slots). This will ensure that your weaving will be centred on the loom.

Untie the left-hand bunch of threads. Take the first two threads from the left of the cross sticks and thread through the first slot of the heddle. This double thread forms the selvedge.

Take the next thread from the cross and thread through the adjacent hole on the heddle.

Repeat across the heddle untying each bunch in turn and taking the threads in order from the cross sticks – one thread in a slot, the next in a hole. Finish with the last two threads together to form the other selvedge. It is essential to take the threads in the correct order off the cross sticks to maintain the correct plaid pattern.

When the whole warp has been threaded, take a further thin stick and tie to the cloth beam either with cords or the ties of the canvas apron. To tie the warp to the stick that is attached to the cloth beam (cloth stick), divide the threads into bunches of 20 again. Split each bunch in half and tie the threads in an overhand knot to the cloth stick as shown (figs. 16, 17, and 18). Make sure that the bunches of threads are evenly tensioned. Untie the rigid heddle so that it is free to move up and down to make the sheds.

Weaving the scarf

Once the warp has been put on the loom, half the fabric has been made. To create the plaid pattern, you must follow the weaving order of picks in fig.19. The colours in the warp combine with the colours in the weft to give the pattern.

Wind up a stick shuttle with the black yarn. Push down on the heddle. Half of the warp ends will be separated from the others forming your first shed. Lift up the heddle so that the other set of warp ends is now above and you have your second shed.

Use the heddle as a beater to push the weft into place. Do not forget that, unlike tapestry, the warp must not be completely covered and there should eventually be an even warp to weft ratio. The rules about tension still apply and you should still take your weft thread across the warp in an arching loop so that your fabric will consistently measure 29cm (11½in).

After six picks of black, break off the black yarn and change to the red yarn, the next colour in the plaid.

Follow the weft chart (see fig.20) until you cannot weave comfortably. Stop weaving and wind the woven fabric onto the front roller (cloth beam). The warp sticks should be wound in with the cloth as they are removed from the warp beam (see fig.16). This prevents the knots from affecting and distorting the fabric.

Finishing off

When you have completed the pattern and your scarf measures 140cm (56in), unroll the cloth beam and remove the sticks. Untie the warp from the cloth stick. Remove the warp from the warp stick (the stick attaching the warp to the warp beam) and cut the loops. Slip off the rigid heddle.

Divide the warp ends into bunches of six (seven at each end) and tie in an overhand knot. Trim the fringe and darn in the weft ends.

The illustrations opposite show how to wind in the warp sticks, and how to tie the threads to the cloth stick.

15. Wind sticks in with warp
16. Take bunches under stick.
17. Bring each bunch under stick
18. Tie bunches together

Below: Repeat pattern unit for weft

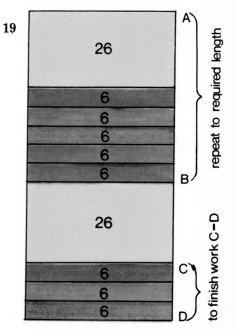

19

26

6

6

6

6

6

26

6

6

6

A

B

C

D

repeat to required length

to finish work C–D

Introducing table looms

The popular table loom may look more complicated than any loom discussed so far but, in fact, the mechanism simplifies and quickens the weaving process while opening up a whole new world of fabric design. The basic weaving principles, of course, remain the same. As in the roller loom, the warp of the table loom is stored on rollers to be unwound as needed but extra equipment exists on a table loom to make the process of weaving easier.

Heddles Instead of the rigid heddle, the table loom has a series of wire or string leashes. These are known individually as heddles or healds. Sets of heddles are attached to movable frames called shafts. The heddles can slide along the shaft and each heddle has an eye through which one warp thread is passed. Each shaft, therefore controls a certain set of warp threads.

The shafts are raised by means of a simple lever system. As the shaft is moved it raises its heddles which in turn pull up the threads, thus forming a shed automatically.

Sheds When only two sheds are available, as with the roller loom, the basic plain weave structure of under one, over one is the only weave possible. The table loom with more than two shafts can make more than two sheds as shafts can be lifted either on their own or in combinations. On a four-shaft loom, for instance, lifting shafts individually gives four sheds, lifting them in pairs gives six sheds and lifting in threes gives another four sheds. All the sheds will create a completely different effect as different threads are lifted. The pattern variations available for designing lengths of cloth are therefore endless.

The reed The other major difference between the table loom with shafts and the simple roller loom is that the table loom has a movable framed comb or reed that spaces and spreads all the warp threads. Each tiny space in the reed is known as a dent. The frame of the reed is the batten. It is with this that cloth is beaten down.

Opposite: Alison Mitchell, a professional weaver, works on her 16-shaft loom.

Buying a table loom

When selecting a table loom, you must always bear in mind not only the actual weaving you will want to do but also the space

needed to accommodate the equipment.

So decide first on the space available, and then consider what type of loom to buy. This must be thought of very carefully, as you cannot adapt a loom by adding extra shafts and you must select the loom to suit your particular aims and aspirations.

Two-way loom: if you are only going to weave small items such as scarves, table mats, shoulder bags etc, this calls for a two-way loom rather like the roller loom shown in the last chapter.

There is one very important point to remember if weaving on a two-way loom. The loom takes some time to thread so if making something short such as the scarf, it is a good idea to put on a long warp for several similar articles at the same time. This saves time as you will only have to thread the loom once. The two-way loom obviously restricts you to the basic under one, over one of plain weave and for more interesting patterns, a more versatile loom with more than two sheds is needed.

The four-shaft loom: the next choice of loom is possibly the most popular loom for home use – a four-shaft table loom. These are available in sizes from 30cm to 80cm (12in to 32in) weaving widths. Above this width your arms would become very extended and the pleasure of weaving would be lost.

The size of the loom you choose is very much governed by available space but remember that it is not economical to buy a small loom at first and to discover you need a larger one later. The most popular size is 61cm (24in) weaving width. These looms are capable of weaving tweeds to finish at 55cm (22in) and, of course, all the smaller items already mentioned can be woven. Because you can raise the shafts singly or in any combination you choose, you now have fourteen sheds instead of two. This means that patterns on four shafts are so varied that you could spend a lifetime of home weaving without duplicating a pattern.

If the loom has steel shafts, wire heddles and chains to lift the shafts, carpeting and rugs as well as cloth can be woven to 60cm (24in) width in an infinite variety of patterns.

There is only one limitation on the 61cm (24in) loom which affects the home weaver. This is that tweeds for men's suitings cannot be produced on it. If you want to weave for men's clothes, wider fabric will be required – you will need an 80cm (32in) loom.

Of course, a loom of this size becomes a very static piece of equipment taking up a lot of room. However, weaving on a loom this size which has lifting levers in the front central position is quite a joy. It is generally accepted that the larger the loom, the easier it is to operate and the better the work coming off the loom.

Large looms also mean heavy construction which allows one to

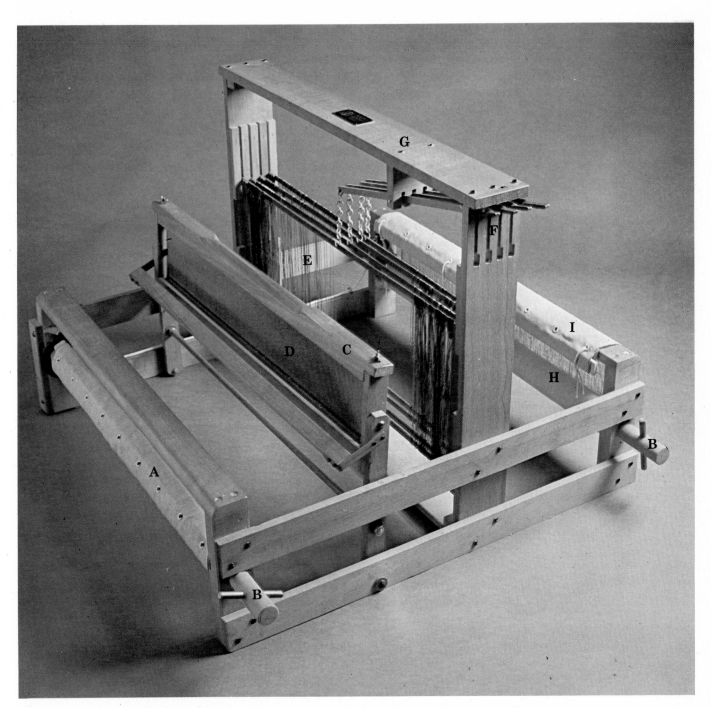

weave very good rugs of carpet wool, either flat kelim rugs or the well-established rya-type pile rug. Even a rug made using unspun wool can be coped with. Small looms cannot accept the bulkiness of these rugs around the cloth beam.

Weaving on a table loom

You have now been introduced to the table loom and its very special vocabulary. Threading up a table loom may look an imposing task to the beginner but, in fact, if you have followed the instructions on making a warp and threading up the roller loom for the plaid scraft you are well on your way to designing your own exclusive fabrics.

The poncho

This is an excellent first project to make on a table loom as it is simply made up from two perfectly straight pieces of weaving (fig.1). The design, shown in the photograph, is in plain weave and made up from botany wool for warmth and extra softness. As you get more proficient and confident about weaving on a table loom, you will be able to create garments in more complex weaves and in an endless variety of patterns.

The loom The basic four-shaft 60cm (24in) width loom is used as a model *for weaving the wool poncho shown here.* If you have a loom that is wider or with more shafts you obviously have no problems and instructions are given throughout this chapter to guide you on your way. However, if you have a loom which is narrower than the weaving width of an article – 45cm (18in) for the poncho – you will have to weave in strips and sew them together to make the pattern pieces. This will obviously be less successful. If you have a two shed roller loom you can still make up the poncho as plain weave only needs the two sheds. Follow the instructions on threading the roller loom that are given for weaving the plaid scarf and ignore those that appear in this chapter which directly relate to the four-shaft loom. Remember that the rigid heddle has 13 not 12 dents per 2.5cm (1in) and extra threads will have to be warped to make up the total number of threads for the required width of the poncho fabric.

The pattern To make the poncho you will need to weave two wool pieces of identical size. For an adult this would be two pieces 45cm by 82cm (18cm by 32½in) when taken off the loom. If you wish to alter the size, be very careful to alter all the instructions

Poncho

You will need :
50g (2oz) pale blue 3-ply wool.
250g (9oz) navy blue 3-ply wool.
75g (3oz) green 3-ply wool.
Four-shaft table loom with a 12 dent reed and a weaving **width of at** least 45cm (18in).
Stick or boat shuttle
Warping pegs and G-clamps [C-clamps] or warping board
Threading hook and reed hook.
At least 12 warp sticks
15mm by 6mm (⅜in by ¼in) but the width of the warp beam on the inside of the frame.
Raddle.
Cotton twine or strong string and scissors.
Stiff brown paper.
Tape measure.

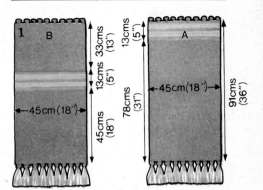

Above: The pattern for the poncho pieces. Off loom length is 82cm (32½ in).

relating to numbers of threads and heddles on each shaft.

As the pattern for the warp threads is completely plain and exactly the same in both pieces, only one warp needs to be put on the loom and the two pieces woven in succession with a 25cm (10in) gap between them for fringes.

The warp

The final length of each piece of weaving is 82cm (32½in). To compensate for take up on the loom and shrinkage with washing, the 'weaver's yard' must actually be woven. This means that for each 90cm (36in) of weaving, 10cm (4in) extra must be woven to allow for this shrinkage. Therefore, each pattern piece of the poncho needs an extra 9cm (3½in) of weaving and each pattern piece will actually be woven 90cm (36in) long.

In addition, 45cm (18in) must be added to the warp for tying up and for the area which cannot be woven beyond the reed. The poncho also needs some warp for fringing at one end of each piece of weaving. Add on another 25cm (10in) fringing before the first piece of weaving. The fringe at the end of the second piece can be made out of warp waste beyond the reed. Finally, a gap of about 25cm (10in) must be left between the two pieces of weaving.

Therefore, for the poncho you will need a warp of 82cm (32½in)

2. One type of warping board. Pegs are removable so that you can use any combination for making long or short warps.

3. By making a raddle cross it is easier to thread the raddle.

4. Cross-section of the warp beam with the warp threads being wound on. Warp sticks should be inserted between the roller and the threads to keep the layers of threads separate and to prevent the unwoven warp from being distorted by the roller.

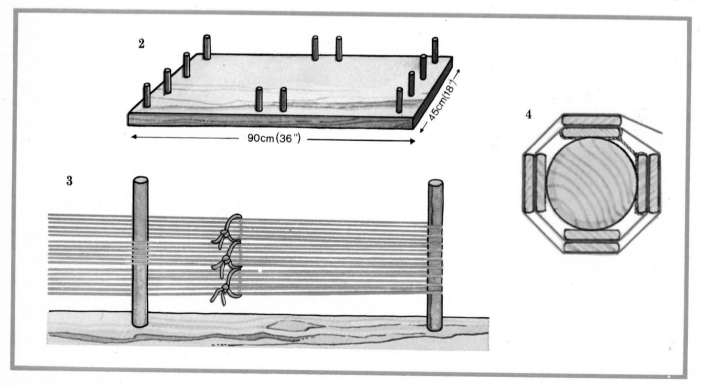

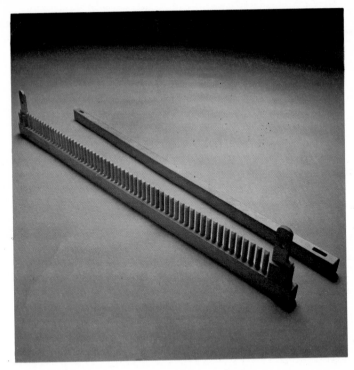

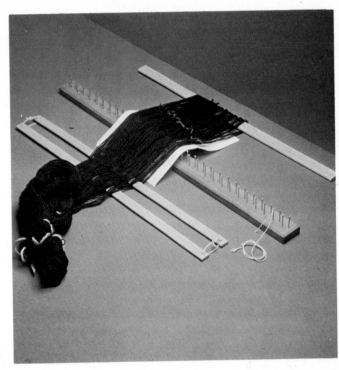

Above left: Top of raddle
prevents threads escaping
Above: Putting batches of threads
in the raddle spaces.

plus 82cm (32½in) plus 18cm (7in) for actual weaving, plus 45cm (18in) for tying up and the warp that cannot be woven beyond the reed, 25cm (10in) for fringing and 25cm (10in) for the gap between the two pieces of weaving. This gives a total of 277cm (110in).

Width of warp The weaving pieces are 45cm (18in) wide and the reed is 12 ends per 2.5cm (1in). The number of threads will be 12 multiplied by 18 which is 216. In addition, this particular design has a firm selvedge. To achieve this you will need not one but three extra threads on each side. Therefore, the total number of warp threads is 216 plus 6 making 222.

Making the warp Make a warp of 222 threads each 277cm (110in) long. Although it is perfectly feasible to make a warp of this length using warping pegs and a table, you may prefer to invest in a proper warping board that can either be kept flat or hung on a wall (fig.2). This piece of equipment makes it possible to make very long warps as well as short ones without monopolizing vast areas of the kitchen table. The dowel pegs in the board are removable and the warp journey can be extended by winding around extra pegs.

Raddle cross As well as making the all-important cross in the warp that gives you the under/over sequence when threading, you may also find it helpful to make another cross at the opposite end of the warp. Make the cross in batches of six threads (fig.3), and your raddle threading will be a lot easier. If you do make the raddle or batch cross, remember that the first and last groups of threads must contain the extra threads of the selvedge. Tie around each batch.

Putting on the warp On a table loom with shafts it is advisable to use a proper wooden raddle. Ascertain the centre dent and count out to the dents 23cm (9in) each side of the centre. Mark these two dents with a piece of yarn. After inserting the warp stick and cross sticks, slide the cross sticks down the chained up warp and spread the intervening warp over the raddle protected by a piece of paper. Thread the raddle from one of the dents you have marked, 23cm (9in) from the centre. This will ensure that the warp, and therefore the weaving, is centred so that the loom is kept balanced.

If you have made the raddle cross, you will find that each tied batch will slot into a dent which makes the process considerably quicker. Do not forget that the dent at each end must contain the three extra threads for the selvedge so each end dent will have nine threads. Place the wooden top back in place on the raddle and tie around the raddle so that the top cannot slip off allowing the threads to become displaced after all your hard work.

Move the warp to the loom with the warp stick at the warp beam end and the cross sticks on the warp beam side of the shafts. Tie the warp stick to the warp beam. Tie the raddle to the back frame of the loom so that the threads are brought from the beam over the frame, through the raddle and into the space between the shafts and the back frame of the loom.

Rolling the warp onto the loom. One person should wind the warp while the other holds the warp in tension and clears any tangles.

Wind the warp little by little onto the warp beam and preferably with the help of a friend. One person should wind the beam while the other faces the loom and holds the threads in tension. The first section of warp must have warp sticks inserted to keep the warp evenly in tension. Always make sure that the sticks are directly on top of each other (fig.4). When you have used up all the sticks you can use brown paper between the layers of threads as the warp is being wound on. If you have a large number of warp sticks do not use paper but put in further circuits of sticks after each two complete turns of the warp beam. Whether you use sticks or paper the idea is to keep the threads separate from each other.

Stop winding the warp when it has completely unchained and you have only enough thread in front to go through the heddles and reed and to tie to the cloth beam. At this stage the cross sticks should be eased back through the warp until they are only about 5cm (2in) away from the back of the frame. Make sure that they remain in this position throughout the weaving.

Divide the warp into two equal sections. Tie each half in an overhand knot and cut all the loops. As the warping pegs bend inwards slightly as the warp is made, you will find that the last threads warped will be slightly shorter than the first. This means that you may find the warp is uneven. Trim down and even the warp, cutting off any knots that you may have tied. Before threading the heddles, make sure that you have 54 heddles on each of your four shafts. This will give you a total of 216 heddles, ie the correct number for your threads as the three selvedge threads merely double up in the heddle.

Plain weave

Plain weave is simply over one/under one and therefore you need to thread up your loom so that you can alternately lift the odd and then the even threads when making a shed.

To achieve plain weave on a four-shaft loom, the warp ends are threaded onto the shafts in the order, 1, 2, 3, 4 and the shafts are then lifted in pairs. Shafts are numbered 1 to 4 from the front to the back of the loom. Shafts 1 and 3 lift all the odd threads and shafts 2 and 4 lift the even threads. Obviously, it is possible to produce other types of weave but these would require either a different lifting combination or a different threading. The simplest method is to have all the odd numbered threads on the odd numbered shafts and the even threads on the even shafts.

Entering To thread the heddles, face the loom and take the first two threads on the outside of the right-hand bunch off the cross sticks and thread them through the eye of the first heddle on shaft 1. The two threads form part of the selvedge.

Thread the next two threads through the first heddle on shaft 2 and the next two threads through the first heddle on shaft 3. These three sets of double threads form the selvedge.

Take the next thread off the cross sticks and thread through the first heddle on shaft 4. The next thread from the cross sticks should now go through the second heddle on shaft 1 and so on. Repeat across the warp, taking the threads in the correct order and

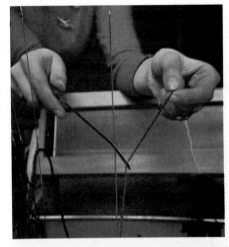

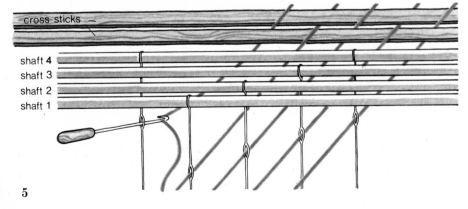

Top: Using a hook to thread the heddle

Above: A reed hook is used to sley the reed.

Left: Threads should be placed onto the four shafts in turn.

5

threading them onto the shafts in a 1, 2, 3, 4 order (fig.5). Make sure that the threads come off the cross sticks in the correct order and that all the over threads go onto one pair of shafts while all the under threads go onto the other pair of shafts.

Threading hook If you have difficulty threading the heddles with your fingers, a threading hook should be used instead. Push the hook through the eye of the heddle, catch your thread and pull it through the heddle.

When you have finished threading the right-hand bunch of threads start threading the left-hand bunch remembering to continue with the 1, 2, 3, 4 sequence. When you have only the last six outside threads left, thread them in pairs onto the last heddle on shafts 2, 3 and 4. This completes the threading.

If you think that you have made a mistake in the threading up, check that you have not missed out either a thread or a shaft in the threading process.

The reed

The reed controls the sett or spacing of the threads just as the nails did on the tapestry frame. Because different setts are needed for different fabrics, reeds are available in different sizes. For the poncho a 12-dent reed is recommended. However, if you have a roller loom with a rigid heddle then the 13 dents per 2.5cm (1in) of the heddle will produce a slightly firmer fabric as there are more threads to each 2.5cm (1in) square.

Reeds can be used for more than one spacing as threads can be doubled up or dents can even be missed out.

For instance, the 12-dent reed can be used for: 6 ends per 2.5cm (1in) by threading every other dent; 12 ends – every dent; 18 dents – one thread and two threads alternately; 24 ends – two threads. If it can be avoided, try not to leave empty dents and it is strongly advised that you gradually build up a collection of reeds for different density fabrics.

Threading the reed When all the heddles have been threaded, the warp has to be entered through the reed. This process is known as sleying and a special reed hook makes it easy.

Mark the centre of your reed and face the loom. Push the reed hook through the centre dent and pick up the centre thread on shaft 1. Working in either direction, enter all the threads in the correct order of the shafts. Remember to follow the order 4, 3, 2, 1 from right to left and 1, 2, 3, 4 from left to right.

When you come to the last threads which have been threaded double through the heddles, treat them as one thread and place the doubled threads through one dent of the reed.

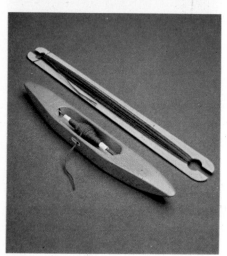

Top: Threading hook and reed hook
Above: Boat shuttle and stick shuttle

6	2.5cm (1″)
	12mm (½″)
	} 12mm (½″)
	2.5cm (1″)
	} 12mm (½″)
	12mm (½″)
	2.5cm (1″)

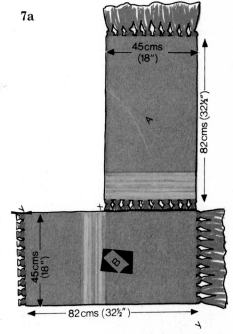

Tying on When all the threads have been entered through the reed, tie the warp threads into groups of about 20. Remove the raddle and tie the warp onto the front beam with the apron stick. It is very important to make sure that the warp is evenly tensioned across the full width of the loom.

Roll the cloth beam forward a little to even up the tension of the warp. Do not remove the cross sticks. Before you begin to weave, you should always check to see that you have threaded up correctly by lifting each pair of shafts in turn. Any thread that remains static has obviously not been threaded through a heddle. A tangle between the reed and heddle will result in the cross threads remaining stationary and any mistakes in sleying the reed will be shown in unusually thick or thin areas of threads.

Check carefully for mistakes and make sure that they are corrected before weaving starts or you will have bad flaws in your fabric.

Weaving the poncho

As the poncho has a 25cm (10in) fringe at the beginning, roll 30cm (12in) of warp onto the cloth beam before starting to weave.

Shuttle When working on a wider warp it is much quicker to weave with a proper boat shuttle, although a stick shuttle is perfectly sufficient for most purposes.

The boat shuttle is shaped so that it can slide quickly through the shed when propelled by a push from one hand and caught by the other hand – hence the term 'throwing' the shuttle. Bobbins are contained within the boat shape and rotate as they play out the weft thread. These can be wound either by hand or with a proper bobbin winder but make sure that you do not overwind the bobbin.

Wind up your shuttle or bobbin with the navy blue yarn. Pull the batten forward to clear the shed and return it. Raise shafts 1 and 3 and weave one pick. Raise shafts 2 and 4 and clear the shed with the batten once more ready for the next pick.

Weave one pick and beat down gently with the batten. Leave a loop

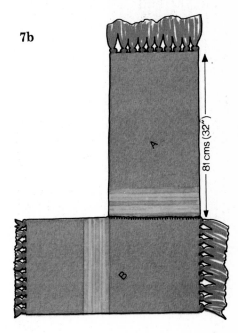

6. Detail of striped area
7a,7b. Positioning and stitching the first seam of the poncho.

7c

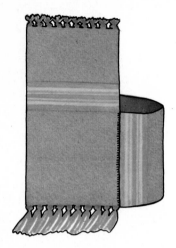

7d

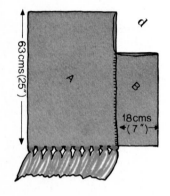

63 cms (25")

18cms
(7")

7c, 7d. Stitching the seams at front and back of the poncho.

so that the weft yarn is not too tight.

Change shed and clear with the batten before weaving the next pick. You will soon get into a rhythm of throwing the shuttle, beating down, changing shed, beating and throwing the shuttle again.

Try to keep the weave as balanced as possible by weaving roughly 11 picks per 2.5cm (1in). When the cloth is taken off the loom it should spring back to give you a perfectly balanced sett.

Weaving the pattern The two pattern pieces have large areas of navy blue with a small 13cm (5in) band of smaller blue and green stripes (see fig.1 and fig.6).

For piece A (see fig.1) weave 78cm (31in) in navy blue yarn. As you get close to the heddles, wind the woven cloth onto the cloth beam placing sticks in with the fabric to keep it smooth. When you run out of sticks use brown paper. Also remember to move the cross sticks backwards when winding on, to ensure that they do not crash into the shafts interrupting the rhythm.

Weave the last 13cm (5in) in the striped pattern, the details of which is shown in fig.6. When you have woven this pattern area you have completed the 90cm (36in) of the first pattern piece. Leave a gap of 25cm (10in) and insert a stick into the shed created by any one shaft. This will secure the stick and you will have something to beat against as you weave.

Start weaving again just above the stick and follow the pattern for piece B (see fig.1). Weave 45cm (18in) in the navy blue yarn. Weave the 13cm (5in) of the striped pattern. Finish piece B by weaving 32cm (13in) in navy blue.

When you have finished the second piece of weaving, unroll the cloth beam and untie the warp from the cloth stick. Remove remaining warp from the warp stick, cut the loops and slide the warp out of the heddles and reed.

Cut the warp area exactly in the middle of the gap so that the same amount of fringe is left on each piece. Trim the warp at the other ends of the pieces to leave 15cm (10in) lengths. Make overhand knots at each end of the poncho pieces.

Making up the poncho The two pattern pieces are joined together so that only one set of fringes from each piece will show.

Place the two pieces on a flat surface in the positions shown in fig.7a. Cut short the fringes at ends X and Y as these will not show. Blanket stitch the two pieces together at X as shown in fig.7b, overlapping piece A 12mm ($\frac{1}{2}$in).

Fold piece A back 18cm (7in) from this seam (fig.7c). Turn the poncho wrong side up. Fold forward 19cm (7$\frac{1}{2}$in) of piece B (fig.7d) and join B to A with blanket stitch again allowing a seam of 12mm ($\frac{1}{2}$in). Press gently before wearing.

Spinning

Spinning with a spindle

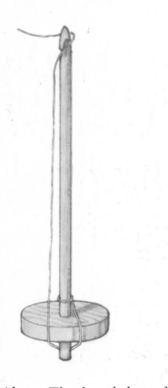

1

Above: The threaded spindle

The art of hand-spinning is still very much alive. Many weavers like to create interesting and unusual yarns for their projects by spinning wool themselves from the raw fleece.

Before the sixteenth century and the invention of the spinning wheel, the spindle was the only equipment generally available for spinning wool. The simple spindle is just a wooden stick with a notch at the top and a disc fixed near the bottom. It is the most primitive of spinning equipment and is especially suitable for beginners as it does not demand considerable skill. Spindles can be bought fairly cheaply from specialist suppliers, but if you have a coping saw and a brace and bit, you can easily make a spindle at home in just a few hours.

To make a spindle

Using the coping saw, make a disc 7.5cm (3in) in diameter. Smooth down the edges with sandpaper. Drill a hole in the centre of the disc using the brace and bit. Push the dowel rod through this hole until a little less than 2.5cm (1in) shows under the disc. If you have made a hole that is too large a little plasticine will hold the dowel rod in place. The hole may need sanding if slightly small. With the knife, cut a notch 2cm (¾in) from the top end of the dowel rod (fig.1). Shape and smooth this end of the dowel rod with the knife and sandpaper, so there are no rough edges to catch the yarn.

Raw materials

As with all crafts, a spinner should gain a good working knowledge of the raw material. Generally, fibres are classified into different categories depending on their origin: animal hairs such as wool, mohair, alpaca and cashmere; vegetable fibres such as cotton, linen (flax), jute and hemp; regenerated fibres such as rayon and synthetic fibres such as nylon. All these fibres can be used by the handspinner but it is wool that is more commonly used, primarily because it is probably the most commonly available and certainly the most varied in both quality and colour.

There are many different breeds of sheep due to very great

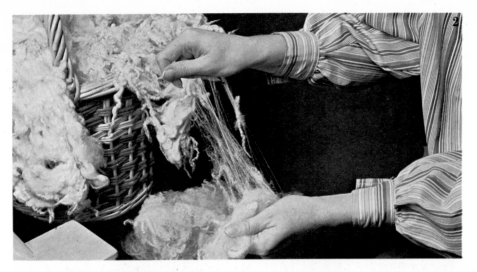

2. *Teasing the fleece*
3,4. *Place fleece on left carder draw right hand carder across.*
5. *Forming a rolag*
6. *Before spinning, 45cm (18in) of yarn must be prepared by hand.*

differences in environment and climate. It is therefore not surprising that sheep wool provides the weaver with a raw material that can be made into fabrics of great diversity in appearance, quality and use. Sheep breeds are classified into three main groups.
Lustre and long breeds generally have wool which is straight fibred, strong, long, of good lustre and free from kemp (hairs).

Mountain and Hill Breeds Wools from this category are liable to be much coarser and contain kemp.

Short and Devon breeds Wools from this category of sheep tend to be short, curly, soft and fine to the touch.

There are two additional classes of sheep or types of wool that are very important because they are well known and very common all over the world, the Merino and Crossbred.

Merino The majority of fine-wooled flocks of the world have been derived directly or indirectly from the Spanish Merino breed which for centuries has been famous for the fineness and excellent quality of its wool. As this sheep responds well to a dry climate, its introduction to Australia was very important. Botany wool, which takes its name for Botany Bay where the breed was first introduced, is a term now synonymous with fineness.

Crossbred This word is used when describing those sheep which have been evolved by crossing one breed with another in order to develop some desired characteristic or combination of characteristics. As in the case of New Zealand sheep, this is often for the benefit of good mutton production. This has an adverse effect on the quality of the wool produced by these sheep.

Comparing fleece By using and comparing different wools you will become acquainted with their many varying qualities. Examine stray wool which is caught on hedgerows or visit other spinners or sheep-shearing events at country shows if possible.

Raw wool can be bought undyed, ready sorted and in small amounts of about 227gram (8oz) suitable for the handspinner. These small quantities are known as matchings and generally graded according to quality. You can also buy commercially prepared fleece ready for spinning. This has generally been washed and combed. Suppliers sometimes list such material in their yarn catalogues as rovings, top or sliver.

A small quantity of fleece should be bought to begin with – about 1 kilogram (2½lb) is recommended. Whole fleeces can also be bought but as they weigh on average about 5 kilogram (6lb) it is best to buy small amounts to practice with. Wool gathered from barbed wire is not always recommended as weathering destroys the essential natural oils. Because sheep vary so considerably the colour and texture of fleece offers a range of choice to the hand spinner.

7

Above: Starting to spin

Opposite: As the spindle is twisted, pull the fibres from the rolag.

Natural colours can range from almost white through cream and brown to the black and white of the Jacobs' sheep. When woven undyed these tones may be used in contrast to produce attractive combinations and subtle contrasts in colour and shading.

Preparing raw wool

The wool must first be teased and carded to separate the fibres and prepared for spinning by forming a roll of wool or rolag. Wool contains natural oils essential to the texture – and the oils should not be washed out of it before the spinning.

To tease wool, take a small amount and gently pull it out until the fibres resemble gossamer (fig.2) and pick out any dirt.

Carding Wool grows on sheep in definite locks or staples. Each staple is made up of many thousands of individual fibres. The natural staples of fibres must first be broken up and mixed thoroughly so that they lie together in a light and fluffy regular mass with the fibres all lying in the same direction. This is done first with the fingers and then with the hand carders.

You will need two carding combs or carders. Modern carders are square hand-held instruments that have a working surface covered with thick cloth or leather through which wire bristles project. The carders separate the fibres by catching them between the bristles. Take one of the carders in your left hand and hold it so that the handle points to the left, away from your body and the wired area towards you and upright (fig.3). With your right hand, spread enough of the teased wool across the teeth of the carder you hold to cover – but only just – the teeth.

Gripping the other carder in your right hand, draw the teeth of the right carder quickly and lightly across the teeth of the lett carder in a circular movement (see fig.4). Keep the left hand steady so that the action of the bristles reduces the fibres to a fine state evenly distributed on both working surfaces of the carder. Repeat this action five or six times. The action pulls all the fibres into a uniform direction and they become much softer. Reverse the action once and the wool will come away from the lower teeth. The resulting mass of fibres should be gently rolled between the backs of the carders into a cylindrical shape called a rolag (fig.5).

Spinning

Before spinning you will need to prepare by hand about 45cm (18in) of woollen thread from a rolag.

Take a rolag in your left hand and with your right pull a few fibres. As you pull them twist them clockwise to form a short thin thread. Secure this small thread on something firm such as a hook

and continue to pull and twist in a clockwise direction using both hands so that the thread grows longer. The thread is very liable to pull apart and break in places. When this happens, overlay the last 2.5cm (1in) with fibres from the rolag, and, while holding the weak point between the left finger and thumb, continue to twist.

The spindle When at last the thread measures 45cm (18in), unhook the end and tie it around the spindle so that it is secured a little above the wooden disc (fig.1). Take the yarn down over the edge of the disc and around the dowel rod. Bring the yarn up over the disc again to the notch at the top of the dowel rod as shown. Secure the yarn around the notch with a knot. The spindle is now ready.

Spinning sequence Place the rolag over the back of the right hand pinching out the thread between the first finger and thumb (fig.7). With your left hand twist the spindle sharply clockwise from the base and making sure that the spindle stays clear of the ground (fig.8). At this point, move the left hand up and pinch the thread a little below the right hand (fig.9). Pull out a few more of the fibres before pinching the thread again and releasing the thread with the right fingers.

The sequence to follow is: Turn spindle, left hand; pinch fibres, left hand; pull out more fibres, right hand; pinch, right hand; release left hand for spinning spindle again. An easy rhythm should emerge with practice. Overlay threads from a new rolag as the first one comes to an end.

As more yarn is spun the spindle will reach the floor. Stop spinning and unhitch the yarn from the top and bottom of the spindle. Wind the yarn around the dowel rod between the disc and the notch, criss-crossing it to form a cone shape so that the spindle is balanced. Leave 45cm (18in) unwound to start the process all over again but make sure that you do not put so much yarn onto the spindle that it will not spin in a balanced way. When the spindle is full, wind the yarn off onto the upright back of a chair leaving 45cm (18in) unwound to start spinning again. Retie this length to the spindle and begin again. Remove the skein and tie loosely in four places.

Washing the wool Before the wool can be made up it must be washed. Prepare a bowl of warm water and add pure soap or soap flakes such as are recommended for washing delicate wool garments. Soak the skeins for twenty minutes, squeeze gently and rinse in warm water. Repeat this three times and after the final rinse, cut the ties and rewind the wool onto the back of the chair to dry and stretch. (Do not use a polished wooden chair unless it is protected by a plastic bag). Do not dry the wool in any heat as it will shrink and become matted into an unpleasant looking mess. The best solution is to dry the wool in a warm, sunny position.

Spinning on a wheel

If you enjoy making yarns on a drop spindle then a proper spinning wheel is the next step. The invention of the flax or long fibre wheel is generally attributed to a sixteenth century German woodcarver. Before this invention spinning was a very slow process. The flax spinning wheel made it possible to both spin and wind on simultaneously, therefore considerably increasing the speed of the whole process. The wheel is fitted with a treadle so the spinner is able to use both hands for controlling the drawing out of fibres from the rolags. This means that not only is the process faster, but because both hands can control the fibres, a finer yarn can be spun.

Although spinning wheels vary a great deal in size and form depending on the country or even district of origin, they all exhibit the same essential features – wheel with foot control, bobbin and spindle flyer where the spun yarn is wound.

Above: The great wheel has no foot control.

Preparing a fleece

If you have invested in a spinning wheel, you will probably wish to buy wool by the fleece. This is the cheapest way to buy wool and is really the best way of seeing your raw material in its proper state, shaped as it is sheared off the sheep. The fleece must be prepared by sorting, cleaning and carding before spinning.

Sorting is the selection of wool from the various areas of the fleece into the best or most useful parts. Obviously the back, sides and shoulders are better quality than the dirtier, coarser belly and haunches (fig.1). In the case of a black and white sheep, sorting may be just separating the two colours.

Testing Raw wool is usually extremely dirty and greasy but do not let this put you off, handspun wool is generally best spun in the oily state. A lot of dirt from the natural fleece can be shaken out and burrs and prickles removed without much trouble. Teasing the fleece should get rid of any dirt. It is advisable to store your fleece in an air-tight bag to prevent it getting dry and brittle.

Dyeing It is best not to wash the natural oils out of wool before spinning but, of course, it must be thoroughly washed if it is to be dyed. This is because the natural oils and grease must be removed

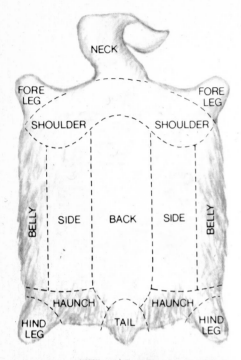

Short and Down type

Lustre type

Mountain type

Top: *The different areas*
of a fleece.
Above: *Samples of different*
wool varieties.
Opposite: *Pictorial montage*
of the world of sheep,
spinning and weaving.

or the oil will repel the dye. This is done by washing the entire fleece using the following recipe:

Wash the wool in 45 litres (10 gallons) of warm water containing 2 litres (60floz) of ammonia and 1 litre (30floz) of liquid soap containing a water softener. Then rinse in warm water and leave to dry. Dye the fleece with a commercial cold water dye or use natural dyes for special soft, earthy colours. When spinning, sprinkle vegetable oil lightly on the fleece before teasing.

Spinning on a wheel

For spinning on a spinning wheel, it is important to prepare a number of rolags to have ready beside you before you start.

The hardest part of spinning for the first time is getting used to controlling the pedal with the foot at the same time as controlling the yarn with the hands. For those used to a treadle sewing machine, the operation should be a lot easier. Before attempting to spin it is wise to practise using the wheel by sitting beside it and getting the feel of the treadle alone. Aim to get the wheel revolving relatively slowly and smoothly. The next step is to get foot and hands working together and this is really a matter of practice. Do not get frustrated at unsuccessful first attempts.

The first stage in the actual spinning process is to tie a piece of strong commercial yarn to the bobbin and one of the hecks or hooks on the flyer arm (fig.2). Then with a straightened out but bent-ended hairpin (kept or tied to the spinning wheel) thread the yarn through the hole in the spindle (fig.2). Now revolve the wheel holding the yarn you have just threaded tightly in your left hand. As you revolve the wheel, the yarn will naturally want to wind on to the bobbin, but hold it firmly and stop it from doing this. As you hold the yarn, the wheel will twist it just as the spindle does when twirled. By holding a rolag ready beside the yarn, the twist will transfer into the drawn out fibres from the rolag. Thus, the spinning process is started in exactly the same way as with the drop spindle with the two yarns twisting together.

While gently but firmly revolving the wheel with your foot, you should hold the twist that is forming between the finger and thumb of your left hand and gently pull and draw out the fibres from the rolag behind it with your right hand. As time and your own competence progress, these two hand movements become one automatic movement of holding the twist being formed and pulling out fibres from the rolag.

The hooks on the flyer arm are to distribute the spun yarn evenly onto the bobbin. As you build up one area, move the yarn along to the next hook so that the next area of the bobbin can be built up.

Above: The standard type spinning wheel.
Above right: Take yarn around the hook and through the hole in the spindle.
Below right: A- flyer; B- bobbin; C- hooks; D- hole in spindle.

Some spinning wheels have a twist bolt positioned underneath the spindle flyer which can be pulled towards or away from the wheel thus tightening or loosening the tension. This in turn controls how quickly or slowly the spun thread is drawn onto the bobbin.

Using your yarn

It is very easy when spinning to produce those bumpy, obviously handspun yarns by pulling out the fibres from the rolag in uneven quantities. Aim to produce an even medium or thin yarn as this will be the true test of your competence.

With practice and skill in using the spindle or the wheel it is possible to produce a yarn suited for weaving both in texture and strength. However, it is hard for the beginner to achieve the uniform tension in the twist that is needed when weaving a fabric totally in handspun yarn. The unevenness and knotted texture of handspun yarn, however, make it an excellent feature in the weft only of either tapestry or fabric weaving. Individual picks or even lengths of unspun fleece can be inserted in the weft and held in position by a couple of rows of plain weave. Some remarkable effects can be achieved with the imaginative use of handspun yarn in combination with commercial yarn. This is why the process of spinning is so highly attractive to the weaver.

Glossary

Beater Any tool which is used to push the weft down into place. Often fork or comb-shaped, but sometimes a plain stick beater is used.

Beating A method of pushing the weft down into place.

Bobbin Used in tapestry work, a specialized tool to carry the weft yarn.

Carding A method of breaking down and mixing fleece fibres so that they lie together in the same direction.

Cheese (also spool, cone, hank, skein) Methods of packaging yarn.

Cross The position in the length of warp where the warp ends are correctly ordered by crossing each successive thread alternately.

Cross sticks Inserted after warp tension has been adjusted, the sticks maintain the order of the threads against the warp.

Finger weaving A process of making woven cloth by using the fingers to guide the weft through the warp ends.

Heddle (heald) Wire or string structure on a table loom with an eye through which a warp thread is passed.

Inkle weaving A method of weaving which produces narrow braid strips.

Leashes Lengths of cotton yarn passed between groups of warps and knotted, which enable the weaver to lift the groups of warp threads quickly.

Loom Any structure, simple or complex, which is devised to hold weaving materials in tension, leaving the hands free for weaving.

Ply (also fold) The number of singles fibres which are twisted together to make yarn.

Raddle Comb-like tool on a roller loom which spreads the warp ends across the correct width, and keeps them in the correct order.

Ratchet A mechanism on a table loom which holds the beams in place and allows them to be unrolled. It also keeps tension on the warp.

Reed A comb-like structure through which the warp threads are passed. The reed spaces the threads to a particular sett, and different reeds are used to create light or heavy fabrics.

Rolag A roll of wool formed after the fleece has been teased and carded, ready for spinning.

Sett The number of warp ends per inch.

Shed The opening made in the warp when a number of warp ends are raised. The shuttle is passed through this opening.

Single One strand of fibre, not plied. It is suitable for weaving lengths of cloth such as tweed, as it imbeds itself with other singles yarns.

Shuttle A tool used to carry the weft.

Tablet weaving A form of warp-twined weaving, in which the warp threads are passed through holes in cards which are known as tablets.

Tapestry A weaving technique which produces pictorial effects, using a special method for joining areas of colour and texture.

Warp The lengthways yarn wound onto the loom. The individual threads are called ends.

Weft The yarns which weave horizontally across the warp.

Index